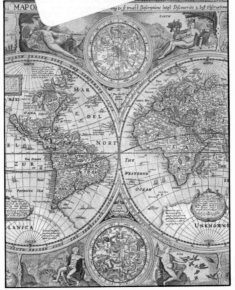

FROM THE LIBRARY OF

Bridget Callais

ALSO BY MARK O'DONNELL

Elementary Education

Plays:

Tots in Tinseltown

Fables for Friends

That's It, Folks!

The Nice and the Nasty

Plays in translation:

A Tower Near Paris by Copi

The Best of Schools by Jean Marie Besset

VERTIGO PARK

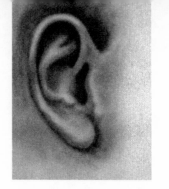

MARK

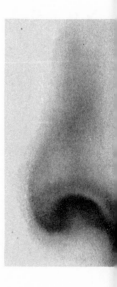

VERTIGO PARK

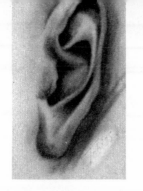

O'DONNELL

and other tall tales

ALFRED A. KNOPF, NEW YORK 1995

This Is a Borzoi Book Published by Alfred A. Knopf, Inc.

Two cartoons, "The Solar Yearbook" and "Extinction of the
Dinosaurs Fully Explained," and one story, "Diary of a Fan,"
were originally published in *The New Yorker*.

Library of Congress Cataloging-in-Publication Data

O'Donnell, Mark.

Vertigo Park : and other tall tales / by Mark O'Donnell. — 1st ed.

p.   cm.

ISBN 0-679-40040-0

I. Title.

PS3565.D594V47   1993

818'.5402—dc20   92-20673

CIP

Published April 19, 1993
Second Printing, April 1993

In memory of Robert Cohen, who will always get the joke

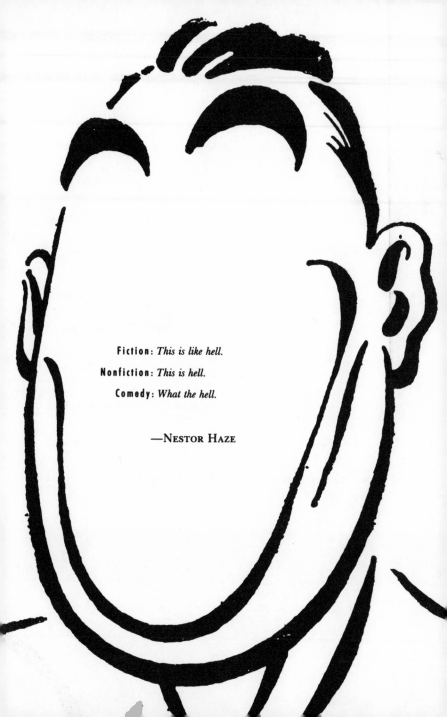

Fiction: *This is like hell.*

Nonfiction: *This is hell.*

Comedy: *What the hell.*

—Nestor Haze

CON

3   Vertigo Park

53   Marred Bliss

67   Questions for Review

81   Three Lost Poems

92   *Illustration Break*

105   The State of the Hate

113   Bartlett's Familiar Quotations: The Play

126   The Art of Fictitiousness: An Interview with Samuel Beckett

137   The Whom of Kaboom, or What Happened to the Shark

TENTS

The Solar Yearbook   50

A Tall Tale   61

The Corpse Had Freckles   69

Diary of a Fan   84

Guess Who's Psychic   100

Kids' Most-Asked Questions About Electricity   110

The Girl Who Dated the Moon   123

Overheard While Walking: Fragments of the Perambulation   134

PARK

VERTIGO PARK

| PROLOG |

It was called Vertigo Park by accident, because
Curtis Wills Booney, its founder, was mistakenly
advised that vertigo meant green. His wife was a
fanciful but dangerously half-educated woman who
admired culture but didn't pay close attention to it,
so when he solicited her suggestions for his planned
utopian community, she turned off the player piano
(having long since despaired of lessons) just long
enough to offer two options—Mount Olympus Valley
and Vertigo Park. In those days women were deferred
to in matters of civic aesthetics, since aesthetics had
no apparent effect on anything. In any case, his

gesture helped her feel more like his muse and less like his nurse, though his nurse is what she was, especially at the end, with his project a doomed folly and him raving in his bathrobe about Tomorrow being late. Mount Olympus Valley he rejected as too pagan (also, the acreage was completely level), and, as pundits were to observe repeatedly later, calling the place Vertigo Park was probably the most appropriate choice.

It had been Booney's vision to build what would have been the very first shopping mall, in an undeveloped outskirt of St. Louis, just outside Pompey, the rubber tire town. Inspired by the isolationist purity of the glass-domed cities of thirties science fiction, Booney imagined an indoor town square complete with a verdant if not vertiginous small park. In his mind a greenhouse roof would keep out the Depression blight and world tension that were raining debilitation like soot on the farms and factories of what was later called the Rust Belt. If St. Louis had been the Gateway to the West, Vertigo Park was to be the Gateway to Tomorrow, but its unfinished shell was already abandoned and corroding when Booney died, in 1939, the year of the New York World's Fair, a more famous version of the same mistaken future.

His heirs, typically, didn't share his obsession, and concentrated instead on preserving the storm-window installation business he left behind, along with the thousands of sheets of glass that were meant to surmount and contain his dream enterprise. In high winds, some of the panes that had been fitted into the colossal iron skeleton would dislodge and shatter on the ground below, leading local mothers to forbid their children to go near the shivering hulk. Nonetheless, the neighborhood that uneasily grew up around it in the postwar boom was still identified as Vertigo Park, in the way an Indian word for a stretch of woodland survives uncomprehended after Indians and woodland have long been superseded by amnesiac tract houses and demoralizing power plants. It was a favorite irony of later decades that Vertigo Park, Mother of Presidents, Birthplace of Our Carlotta, had languished as a failed suburb for years, with even the freeway passing it unacknowledged. It rose from its prenatal grave only as a ghost, as a tourist oddity of the late nineties—the childhood home of two successive U.S. presidents, the two youngest U.S. presidents, the two worst U.S. presidents, the two final U.S. presidents. Even more mythically, it was the birthplace of the suffering first lady they both shared and lost, who brought them more honor than they brought themselves, who passed from triumph to tragedy and on into the torpor of legend. If a gate has only to stand and let events pass through it, then Vertigo Park was the gateway to tomorrow, since the future is only the present left to run wild.

CHAPTER ONE

CARLOTTA BY ACCIDENT

She was named Carlotta by accident, because the immigrant night watchman who found the abandoned newborn in a car lot ran gibbering with her to the local police, crying "Car lotta! Car lotta!" to explain where she'd been. Her birthdate was calculated to be nine months to the day after VJ Day, a product of the victory celebrations in nearby Pompey, people joked. She was the first fruit of peace, with only a surprisingly full shock of blood-red hair to hint at her lineage, and a remarkable stoic quietness that prompted both the desk sergeant and a newly arrested felon to offer to adopt her.

It was settled, finally, that prematurely widowed Almira Hover would raise Carlotta along with her own toddler, Julienne. She certainly couldn't have guessed the two pretty girls would become lifelong partners in rivalry, like salt and pepper—or, more accurately, sugar and saccharine—and incidentally, mascots of modern history. Mrs. Hover (or "Old Mother Hover," as her slicker co-workers called her) was an overwrought woman with a plaintive voice that reminded others of a squeegee cleaning a windshield. She had atoned for whatever passions she possessed, as well as the back-to-back devastations of the Depression and the World War, by scrupulous devotion to the sanitary, an unending ritual of domestic purification as advanced by the women's magazines of the period. Originally she had worked as an assistant to the Ladies' editor at the Pompey *Trumpet*, where her late husband had been a typesetter. His eyesight had been ruined proofreading the minuscule type for legions of classified ads, for the all-but-invisible pleas for Position Sought, Help Wanted, and Home Rummage Sale Extended. Still, he'd managed to be drafted, and astigmatically wandered onto a land mine on Omaha Beach. His death, and her own fetishes, led Almira to become a food stylist, an admittedly limited calling in a small town, but she could assuage her grief and guilt by prettifying party platters for supermarket supplement photos, and, as time went by, for local television. Her duty was not to actual nourishment but to credible appearance on camera, a profession ahead of its time, and in that capacity she became a local character, a media midwife to minor advertising promotions and diner menus.

Like her shellacked turkeys and lard passing for whipped cream, Mother Hover's attempts at nurture were superficially nice and essentially inedible, just as she herself was an imitation rather than a genuine mother to Carlotta. She gave the two girls a love-like substance, but it was a placebo that left its takers restless and with pangs of isolation. They grew up fatherless in an apartment over an unrented storefront, though in her earnest trust in external detail Mrs. Hover festooned the rooms with pipe racks, duck decoys and hunting prints, hoping the tokens of a man around the house would compensate for his absence. Little Julienne and Carlotta guessed something was missing, and later that led them to look too recklessly for salvation in the opposite sex.

Carlotta's childhood was uneventful, as the biographies like to point out. Every night, from her window facing the dark, listless commercial street, she could contemplate the illuminated billboard opposite, an eternally filling glass of milk from an unemptying bottle, a promise of progress and relief that was never quite ready for consumption.

CHAPTER TWO

––––

A BOY CALLED VANILLA

The second baby they found they nicknamed Van, since he was swaddled in an empty vanilla ice-cream tub under the refreshment stand near the abandoned mall. He was further proof that the war had shattered the old morality, and was guessed to be a souvenir of the new, momentarily ecstatic atomic world, the first discharge of the baby boom. He was pale and colicky, a squaller, though beautiful when he finally fell asleep, and his hair was a striking sugary white, as if there had been inadvertent truth in packaging.

Big Bill Walker, a foreman at the tire plant in Pompey, said he would adopt Van. He had nine sons of his own, and claimed one more wouldn't matter. It didn't, which may have been the start of the problem. The Walkers were ruddy, similar beanpoles in descending sizes, like xylophone bars waiting to be struck, uncomplaining workers and draftees who smoked heavily or drove the family station wagon too fast instead of ever defying their father or labor union chapter. Big Bill was a bluff man with thick furrowed brows like hillocks in a country churchyard, and he was so conscientious an official he always insisted his own sons be laid off before anyone else, to show he was no shirker or nepotist. His sons were destined to die in Vietnam, or in industrial accidents, or on vacation, but in any case profusely, across a field of years.

Lost in an already self-effacing crowd, foundling Van grew up impressed by his family's anonymous canine devotion to democracy, and at the same time desperate to distinguish himself. He was christened Christian, since it seemed a likely guess for an un-identified blond, but he was called Van all his life, even on the presidential ballot, and at the end, when the other monks addressed him, though he had taken a vow preventing him from answering. It may have been his perceived duty to vanilla that undid him, trying to be wholesome and popular at the same time.

CHAPTER THREE

———

SON OF DANGER

Cliff knew who his parents were, ironically, because of the three he was the one everyone thought of as a bastard. He certainly behaved with the rudderless ease of one unencumbered with parents. He was named Cliff because his mother had conceived him on the edge of one, overlooking the local lovers' leap. She had gone there near the war's end, despondent over the death of her imagined true love, and there she'd met greasy, lithe Chick Burns, an unlikely lady-killer who'd finally been killed back and figured literal death should follow. Dizzy with the height, the two agreed to make love on the spot, as a farewell to life's absurd sensuality. After their bout, the momentum toward suicide had passed, and when it became clear later that a baby was on its way, they married. This was as impetuous as their lovemaking, because Chick and Kitty—both had had parents who diminished them even in naming them—were as repellent to each other as identical magnets, and they quarreled with the same passion with which they waged sex. Cliff had feral black hair, with a sheen that made it seem blue; he was an alarmingly healthy thirteen-pounder who was two weeks overdue, which may have disposed him to his lifelong habit of showing up late but triumphant.

Before he was five his parents divorced—a greater scandal then—and the sullen handsome boy was shuttled between Kitty's diner and Chick's gas station, which lay on opposite sides of a busy freeway, only a few perilous yards apart. Dangerous as it was, impatient Cliff found it easier to race across the road than to walk a mile down to the pedestrian overpass. His reflexes were good, and he was always lucky.

The diner and the garage were both failures. People resented Chick as they do doctors and lawyers, suspecting he was overcharging them to exploit their ignorance. He wasn't, and this made him bitter. Men assumed Kitty to be of easy virtue because she ran a truck stop. She was, and this made her bitter. The neon signs above their respective establishments were each sadly half missing—her restaurant sign read only RANT, and his garage sign read only RAGE.

Unsupervised, young Cliff entertained himself by jumping on the garage driveway's bell cord, imagining he had the power of a sedan pulling in for more gas. It maddened his father, who occasionally lost customers when he wrongly guessed the bell was just his son pretending to be a car. When he was with his mother, Cliff would drink cup after cup of black coffee, which one truant officer later suggested had made him adult before his time. More likely it was the ill-advised playfulness of the truckers who ate at the diner, teasing his mother with leaden double-entendres and teaching him dirty words as they would a parrot, to laugh when so tiny a thing should pipe up with their own jumbo obscenities.

On either side of the road, Cliff was an outsider, just as Carlotta was in her department-store-window home, and Van—lost in an orphanage-sized crowd —was *e pluribus unum*. It may have been this keen sense of exclusion that governed them and brought them together, and was recognized gratefully by so many millions later on. The ideal of individualism includes an unsounded bass chord of loneliness.

——

CHAPTER FOUR

NOTICED ARE THE NUBILE

Carlotta and Julienne both grew into pretty teen-agers. Carlotta, having come from nothing, de-manded nothing, which gave her a lustrous, accepting quality, as unwittingly seductive as a landscape. Her friendly silence caused the boys at Sacajawea High School to project their fantasies onto her like movies on a blank screen. She was sympathetic, and boys confused that with love. Conversely, though Julienne was beautiful, she made boys think she wasn't. Partly from her inherited faith in falsity, she developed the unconvincing, self-seeking good cheer of a singing commercial. She didn't realize deliberate perkiness offended, the way the smell of ammonia becomes associated with the odors it's supposed to remove. Carlotta waited to see what would happen, whereas Julienne was perpetually tensed for success, like a game-show contestant straining to collect while look-ing good on camera. She knew all the rules, but she still had to fear chance.

However, fate usually withholds destruction until adulthood. Julienne managed to become head cheer-leader at Sacajawea, and had frequent solo yells. She urged her seemingly pepless stepsister to go out for cheerleading too, and was hurt when Carlotta mildly pointed out that it seemed needless and self-involved to her, since sideline activity distracted from the game and didn't help the players except with pressure disguised as love. Julienne was further frustrated by Carlotta when the team members themselves flocked to Carlotta's repose more than to her own obstreperous approval. Carlotta was even drafted to portray the Spirit of Freedom in a school pageant, though she was instructed not to speak. Finally, her driver's ed teacher created a small scandal when he sped off with her during her first lesson, mesmerized by her stoplight-red hair. He was halfway to Chicago before state troopers got him for what only looked like drunk driving.

Worse, or perhaps better, Carlotta attracted the attention of Culvert Booney, son of Vertigo Park's would-be founder, head of the local Legitimate Sons of the Pioneers, and also its best-known playboy. He first noticed Carlotta when she accompanied Mother Hover to the TV studio in Pompey, where she helped Vaseline a roast. A plumpish *bon vivant*, Culvert had found undemanding renown as the local television weatherman. He routinely predicted high winds and frigid temperatures to encourage people to buy storm windows from his family business, and he had done quite well with it, so well that parents were patient with the liberties he attempted with their daughters.

Mother Hover, duly impressed by a celebrity's interest in Carlotta, even an alcoholic like Booney's, invited him to dinner, inexplicably if understandably draping the house in Christmas lights to encourage good feelings. Carlotta responded with innocent indifference, and guilelessly galled Booney by talking throughout the meal about the two boys she had crushes on, student council president Van Walker and poor misunderstood Cliff Burns. Already she was trapped between the antipodal loves that would wrack her life, though she was still too young for full-tilt confusion. Julienne shook with envy to see her ignore an opportunity like Culvert, and Mother Hover served the dessert liqueur in secret despair. Booney drank to unconsciousness, and had to be taken home in a neighbor's car. Although it was a night he would never remember, it was to prove to be a night he could never forget.

| C H A P T E R   F I V E |

THE THREE-HEARTED KNOT

Van did seem to pursue Carlotta, but clumsily and chastely, convinced as if by an imaginary friend that she was the cure for his unhappiness. Although an honor student with good teeth, his will to virtue stymied and bemused people; his first major act after reaching puberty was to announce his vegetarianism and lie down naked in the neighborhood butcher shop window. It was meant to be an evocative protest, but made him better known as an exhibitionist than a moralist. Then, in his search for athletic activity that wouldn't pit man against man or get anyone dirty, he tried to organize a synchronized swimming team at Sacajawea, though no one else would participate. Nevertheless he persisted, swimming for hours every evening in the school pool, perfecting routines for scores of nonexistent teammates, and he often recruited Carlotta to help him time a particularly complex sequence.

She respected Van's feverish idealism, but she was more romantically drawn to Cliff, regally brooding and commanding, despite the widespread presumption he was to be a failure. He became particularly notorious after desecrating a supposed miraculous image of the Virgin's face, which some perceived at a certain angle in the rust stains on a local septic tank. Righteously annoyed, he threw red paint on it, simultaneously obscuring the local chamber of commerce's hope that the image would become a tourist attraction. People gossiped even more nervously when Culvert, jealous of Cliff's place in Carlotta's affections, one day in a hungover haze offered him a hundred dollars to pedal his bicycle into the path of an oncoming truck. Cliff was used to dodging traffic, and impulsively accepted. At the last second Culvert repented and stopped Cliff, promising him the hundred dollars anyway. However, Cliff was intrigued and went ahead with the stunt, spinning nearly sideways under the truck's high chassis, amazingly without injury. Carlotta perceived in both these incidents a holy misfit's honor, unaware that it was more likely a delinquent's stupid compulsion.

One fateful night of their senior year, Van's, Cliff's, and Carlotta's destinies became permanently knotted. It was a warm autumn night, and Carlotta didn't accompany Van to his self-appointed swim practice, but instead rendezvoused secretly with truant Cliff in the school parking lot, where he set off some illegal fireworks he'd stolen. They also made love, her first experience, and its clumsy danger on the concrete, surrounded by a dazzling bower of sparklers and links of firecrackers, excited her. Tragically, one errant rocket went through an open gymnasium window and struck Van in the heel as he was preparing to dive, temporarily crippling him and permanently ending his hopes for a swimming career. People later said his limp was the most interesting thing about him, but when Carlotta found out what had happened, she was from that moment locked into her lifelong dilemma—guilty about Van's wounded goodness, and guilty about Cliff's compelling antisociability. Van was hers but wasn't there. Cliff was there, but was not to be had. Her heart went out fearfully to both of them.

CHAPTER SIX

——

THIN AIR AT HIGH ALTITUDES

Mother Hover knew Carlotta was precipitously close to being in love with Cliff when the girl started coming home exhausted and smelling of gunpowder. In an uncharacteristically ingenious moment, like those adrenalized mothers who can suddenly lift autos off their trapped children, she convinced the alcoholically amnesiac Culvert Booney that he had had his way with Carlotta the night of the harmless Christmas light-decked dinner, and he must pay for her to go away and resolve her resulting pregnancy. Culvert remembered nothing, but in a twinge of retrospective satisfaction and remorse, took Mother Hover's word for it. He gave her a large sum of money, which she announced was a scholarship to acting school for Carlotta, who had just impressed everyone playing Sacajawea, again wordlessly, in the Lewis and Clark float on Homecoming Day. Dishonestly, the money was used for exactly its announced purpose, and Carlotta, unaware of the deception, was packed off to New York City to study. Mother Hover felt guilty but relieved, having successfully bluffed her way through blackmail. Julienne now had her own room in which to chafe. Only after Carlotta left did people notice that Cliff had disappeared. Chick and Kitty each assumed he'd been staying with the other. The kindest gossips theorized he'd enlisted for service in Vietnam, but no one could imagine him taking orders from anybody. Van, meanwhile, recuperated from his leg injury by sorting through scholarship offers from numerous colleges and singing in his clear tenor for the other patients in his wing.

In New York, Carlotta studied Acting Natural and Advanced Simplicity with Nestor Haze, a toweringly avuncular and cagily cornball old writer who had become an institution spinning jingoistic western novels and plays, including a movie about the Alamo that so stirred audiences that war was declared on Mexico as a result, which led to its conversion to our fifty-first state. He taught to keep his ego inflated on a daily basis, and because subservient young people were a fetching distraction from his typewriter. His students were generally aimless offspring of the famous, and here Carlotta met Shep Woodhead, an amiable and talentless nonentity who happened to be the son of an undistinguished president and the grandson of a great one, "Roaring Twenties" Woodhead, who is remembered for saying "Without American business, there would be no American pleasure." Shep had not been called on to grasp business, but he knew his pleasure, and, typically smitten with Carlotta, took her to the hottest zebra-skin-hung and strobe-lit spots, happily dizzying her, if not quite winning her. At discotheques like the Go Go Stop and the I Love You Club, she began to catch producers' eyes, and her luxurious red hair became a flattering banner for the nightclub set. Shep took her into men's rooms to do cocaine while his bodyguards stood outside. He took her upstate to the family home on Paradox Lake, though she mistakenly thought it was called Paradise Lake until the ancient former first lady corrected her, explaining that flooding from higher ground made its water flow in contradictory directions. Carlotta was mortified to have erred before a celebrity, but old Mrs. Woodhead assured her many people thought Paradox was Paradise. When Shep asked Carlotta if she liked sailing, she said she was willing to.

Meanwhile, Van was ascending, too. He won a scholarship to prestigious Leeward College, whose motto was To Stand and Mingle. Founded in colonial times as a divinity school, but latterly a trainer of businessmen, its dull brick buildings were as ponderous and maroon as unabridged dictionaries, and its endowment as vast and slow as that symbol of conservatism, the elephant. Here Van majored in government under the influence of a new set of friends, brash scions of Potency, or anyway, Solvency. His mentor at the Snake Club and the campus *Vox* was Win Woodhead, Shep's antithetically brilliant twin brother. Generally, Win was cynical about the world, which study showed to be wicked, but he was fascinated by Van's malleable virtue and cream-colored bangs. His father had rejected him for not being as cheerful as doggish Shep, and Win, in a combination of homosexual love, spite, and vicarious ambition, decided to mold Van into a future president. Van idolized Win's savvy, and, like Carlotta, was mesmerized by the Woodheads' money-salted mystique. He acceded uncomfortably to Win's well-managed seductions, regarding their affair as a required course, but he was erotically indifferent. Virtue is not a virtue in bed. Gradually Win shifted his hopes for Van from Lover to Lifelong Project, which was after all only a slight adjustment.

His subjugation to Win might have explained Van's strange behavior during his occasional visits to Carlotta in New York, during which their mutual uneasiness was mistaken for a budding relationship. Each wanted to want the other more than they did, though they honestly shared the bond of orphans who witness each other's rise in the world. As both grew busier and more popular in their respective circles, it was harder for them to get together, and that let them assume their love was unchanging.

After graduation, Win engineered a high-paying job for Van at the Acquittable, the Woodheads' huge New York–based insurance company. The job was crunching numbers, truly crunching numbers, human suffering compacted like trash into cubes of data, and it strengthened his resolve to relieve mankind and get noticed at the same time. True to their platonic course, Van moved to the city just as Carlotta was taken to Hollywood. She had excelled in her flat line readings of Nestor's dustbowl ingenues, and he recommended her when a studio sought to film his loose retelling of the Wright brothers' flight called *Woman in Jeopardy*. She was renamed Charlotte Haven, since "Carlotta" sounded overweight, and Haven is better than Hover. Her screaming in the picture—she dangled from a biplane while circling an active volcano—struck a responsive chord in audiences currently frightened by an unaccountable string of plane crashes. The picture was a sleeper hit, and Carlotta's new-found agent, Jay Newfound, set her up for a string of pictures in which she would scream. She wanted to be happy, but she had been typed otherwise.

Carlotta's unsought success led her to a difficult showdown with Julienne, who had taken the train to Los Angeles in her evening gown, hoping to emerge as a rival talent to her stepsister. Julienne assumed bitter feuding between them would attract the most publicity, and she was right, except Carlotta insisted on trying to reconcile, even insisting Julienne move in with her, which threw love's wet blanket over the proceedings, and the press turned away. Julienne bitterly sipped champagne in Carlotta's guest bungalow, acting as if she were plotting her next move.

Then Carlotta's goodwill turned inadvertently fatal.

She brought Mother Hover out from Vertigo Park to live with her, but the superficial glories of Carlotta's glittering house so thrilled and overwhelmed Mother Hover that she died of a heart attack ten minutes after her arrival. Julienne, eager to pin her agitation on external events, and undone by weeks of champagne, blamed Carlotta for their mother's death, and after accusing Carlotta of everything she feared in herself, ran widdershins around the far side of the pool house, and disappeared.

Carlotta had to return to Vertigo Park alone for Mother Hover's funeral. Julienne had appeared to vanish, so to speak; even after all this time, no one knew where Cliff was, except he was rumored to have joined the Hell's Angels; and the town itself seemed in its wan decay about to fade from sight—so Carlotta was grateful when faithfully visible Van showed up at the service. One of the Walker sons had been killed in Vietnam, so Van was torn between two coincidentally simultaneous funerals. Carlotta was flattered that he chose to be at her side, but she noticed he fidgeted throughout the service, in the way men do when they make a decision and then fear it's the wrong one. He looked handsome in his dark suit, though, and Leeward had certainly taught him to mingle smoothly, even in somber situations. After Van finally reverted to his own family's gravesite, Carlotta found herself suddenly confronted with revived advances from Culvert Booney, who assumed Hollywood had rinsed her of all inhibitions. Like the detested formal clothes of childhood, though, which are merely pathetic when unboxed years later, too tiny to be forced to wear, this once imposing figure seemed quaint and helpless, almost suckling as he sought a kiss from her. She had offered him a ride in the dark sanctum of her rented limousine, and when she rebuked his advances, Culvert angrily reminded her of what she had never known, that he believed he had once slept with her, and that he had paid for her to go away to avoid a scandal. Carlotta was boggled and sickened to realize Mother Hover's darkest secret, especially only minutes after burying her, but she rallied—mourning dress gave her dramatic strength—and told Culvert the truth. He was shattered to learn of his own innocence, and even when she offered to pay him back, he could only murmur that he never suspected such things hadn't gone on.

Disillusioned and unnerved, Carlotta phoned Van seeking comfort, and he gladly rushed to her hotel room from the crowded Walker memorial party. She had never wanted him to hold her before, but both were dangerously vulnerable and proximate. Necessity is the mother of affection. They entwined like the babes in the woods, but the next morning, each returned to their subsuming daylight roles. She was determined to find the vanished Julienne, and he to find himself through selflessness.

——

CHAPTER SEVEN

TERROR BENEATH THE GRAPES

Win Woodhead was politically ambitious, but he rightly reckoned his disdainfulness made him unelectable, so he decided to get Van appointed to the National Safety Council. It appealed to Van's idealism, and was a natural promotion from his statistical tasks at the Acquittable. Win presented Van to President Miles Phaeton Torque, who recognized Van's niceness as a flavor missing from the spice rack of his staff. Van got the job, and quickly made headlines when he refused to attend the President's second inaugural gala on the grounds that the energy required for the First Lady's float was excessive. The subsequent blackout of the East Coast confirmed his concern, and the tabloids were soon filled with pictures of Van personally changing citizens' fuses or putting poisons out of reach of children.

In Hollywood, Carlotta's distracted search for her stepsister impaired her performance in her second film, *Centrifugal Force*, which by the laws of criticism was bound to disappoint anyway. She did learn that Julienne had worked for a time as a clothes-check girl in a wild nightspot, and one day recognized her as the poster girl for an X-rated movie called *Will Wanda Never Cease?* Tracking her from these clues, she found out that Julienne had renamed herself Comet and joined a sex cult living in a bankrupt vineyard in the Sonoma Valley. This was a time when cults were in blossom. Carlotta borrowed Nestor's luxuriously refitted pickup truck and drove north.

Once on the vineyard property, Carlotta was captured by the dimwitted gardener, whom Carlotta recognized to her fright as Shep Woodhead, drug-addled, sunburned, and brainwashed to boot. He had dropped out of sight the previous year, and his family had felt looking for him might be too intrusive. He had come to California, since the picnic table called America is on a slant, and everything loose rolls there. His job was to pick up the empty liquor bottles, used syringes, and soiled lingerie that littered the grounds, and he was the only man in the cult besides its leader, the polygamous Pan the Man. Carlotta was further thrown when she was brought by torchlight before the commanding figure of Pan the Man, and he was the runaway Cliff Burns. After a stint as a biker and stuntman, he had discovered his charisma's uses, and had set up his own community, which people pointed out later showed he was presidential material. Julienne was indeed there. She, too, loved Cliff, but was forgotten among dozens of his followers.

As always, Carlotta was thrilled by Cliff, but she knew there could be no trustworthy romantic alliance with him. Still, she was dizzied when he took her hand and walked her through the lush but untended arbors. The moonlight made his totalitarian idyll seem more benign, and she lost her reasoning in the leafy maze of the dark vineyard. Somehow she succumbed to his immediacy a second time, again under stars scattered like loose change on God's night table. Instead of fireworks, this time Cliff spiced his excitement by making love to her on the highway just beyond the gate. Luckily, no traffic passed while they were briefly forgetting their safety rules.

Afterwards, Carlotta's feelings were mixed, so mixed that they were about to spill. In the American tradition, there was a competing cult at the next bankrupt vineyard down the road, a group called the Dionysians, an order of deranged pockmarked men who were supposed to be ecstatic from alcohol but still seemed to brood over neighbor Cliff's success with women. As it happened, man was landing on the moon for the first time that night, and the Dionysians had hallucinated the need to appease the moon with a female sacrifice. Two of its members, the two most able to walk, saw Carlotta in the road and seized her. They didn't see Cliff, though. He carried a gun in the bathrobe he wore, and shot both men dead before they could drag Carlotta more than a few yards. She was unharmed, but her left cheek had been slashed with a knife. Even though man landed on the moon that night, the attack was still a major news story.

Cliff was hailed as the rugged landowner who had saved a movie star's life. Since his cult was all women, it was depicted by the press as a nest of pacific earth children, whereas the Dionysians weren't just drunk and deranged, they were pockmarked. It was roundly concluded that no deliberation would be necessary to declare Cliff not guilty of manslaughter. Shep's parents, who had finally tried but grown tired of looking for him, reclaimed him promptly, and enrolled him at Lilly Willow, a patrician old rehabilitation center.

The public thrilled to Carlotta's escape from death, and warmed to the fact that she had found her lost sister at last. Julienne, upstaged at her own rediscovery, despondently retreated to Vertigo Park to dispose of her mother's and imaginary father's belongings. Cliff was sought by numerous clubs, employers, and advertisers who wanted to borrow his presence to defend the right to bear arms or to endorse a spark plug. It all sounded too much like school, though, and he did nothing, instead taking off in Nestor's fancy truck for days at a time, returning only to descend on Carlotta some dusk, a craggy Cupid surprising Psyche.

Carlotta's publicized suffering made her exempt from ever receiving bad reviews again. Her scar gave her superficial depth, and overlooking it gave her public a smug sense of broad-mindedness. Her next film, *Blood Pressure*, again written for her by Nestor, presented her as a helpless call girl who refuses to entrap a liberal politician for the greedy colleagues who fear him. The apparent corruption of President Torque's administration made the government a convenient villain for even the lightest entertainments. Nestor preserved her image by making this the call girl's first job, and people began to refer to her as Our Charlotte.

CHAPTER EIGHT

PRESENTING THE WIND

Two more Walker sons died in Vietnam, but these deaths were surprising, because the war there had been over for several years. Van's investigation showed that the costly Ace of Spades helicopters in which both had crashed were carelessly manufactured by Woodhead Paper and Aircraft, the source of Shep and Win's trust fund. A nervous stockholder, President Torque promoted Van to National Safety Adviser and called for full disclosure. Win continued to manage Van, indifferent to any potential distress the investigation might cause his family. Soon people were jokingly threatening to have each other investigated by Van Walker, and Win also convinced him to write a very thin book called *Why Not Answers?* which commendably, if vaguely and briefly, called for a return to idealism. It was a bestseller, and the National Council of Mothers declared Van their official choice for son-in-law.

Carlotta, meanwhile, was increasingly unnerved by Cliff's irregular midnight appearances at her house, and debated whether or not to demand his phone number and address. Although he resisted all employment, Cliff did agree to appear in a stage show produced by Nestor. He said he felt guilty about stealing Nestor's truck. It was an improvised monolog, in which Cliff sat and drank a fifth of bourbon, urinated real urine, and fired a real gun at impulsive intervals. No rehearsal was needed, and after leading a cult, Cliff had acquired a taste for commandeering a crowd. The production, called *Manolog*, was a sensation in a small Los Angeles theater. Electrified by a drunken handsome man shooting out lights over their heads, people saw him as a free-living hero, a maverick unfettered by speechifying and special interests. The fact that he never injured anyone intentionally made him seem friendly, and his arbitrary pronouncements suggested a mystic cowboy. Cliff frequently missed performances, which was seen as integrity, and the defiant slap titillated even the stood-up audience. As time went by, however, Cliff became more dependable, and even seemed to look forward to showtime. This confused Carlotta. She wanted to see it as a sign of his socialization, but queasily guessed he was becoming a demagogue. Worse, he was still unpredictable in his visits to her, although he showed up at the theater right on schedule. She phoned Julienne occasionally, hoping to strengthen their bond by sharing her worries, but Julienne tended to insist that a nervous breakdown was what Carlotta needed. Finally, Carlotta gave Cliff an ultimatum— to give her his phone number, and to phone before arriving. He looked at her with cold disappointment, said he thought she knew better than to corral him, and walked out. When he failed to make the next hundred performances of *Manolog*, his audiences concluded that he had disappeared again. They respected his vanishing, though, as if it were duty and not dereliction.

CHAPTER NINE

THE GLORIOUS WEAKLINGS

Van's uncompromising study revealed that the exorbitant slipshod Ace of Spades helicopter had enriched the Woodheads and the Torques, but had caused hundreds of deaths in Vietnam since the war's end. Hounded and impugned, President Torque announced he would show his faith in the accused helicopter by taking a ride in one. Its crash, and his death, threw the nation into an excruciating position, a mood of simultaneous shame and suppressed giggles. Newsmakers pointed out the irony but declined to smile. Spokesmen tried instead to focus on the future, always less shameful or hilarious because it's unknown. A special presidential election was called.

The scandal twisted deeper when it was discovered that the President had committed suicide. The helicopter had been specially built for him to ensure normal operation, and he had tampered with it to ensure its explosion. His Vice President, Price Rice Marmot, committed suicide as well, as a gesture of solidarity with Torque's policies.

Despairing of top officials, the public called for new answers, as if there had been old answers they didn't like. The Republicans perfunctorily nominated ex-president August Dodd Woodhead. The press did make hay of his son Shep being in a drug rehabilitation center, which was a small but at least comprehensible disgrace, but bypassed analyzing the fiscal amoralities of Woodhead Paper and Aircraft as too arcane for cameras. Reporters were merely confused by Win's working for his father's likely opponent, and all Win would say was that someday certain people would be sorry they had ignored certain children. It would have been steering into an already fatal skid to add any more liabilities to August Dodd's campaign, though, since all he could do as Torque's defendant was apologize for an absent monster, take his coat and tiptoe out backwards, hoping for a future invitation for himself.

The Democrats nominated Van. He'd been an orphan, he had no fortune to investigate, and he stood for Examination Before Takeoff. They even excused him for being under thirty-five. Van's slogan was He'll Make Sure It's Right. It was to prove catastrophically true. Win engineered the campaign with virulent resolve, which made Van feel uneasily like a voodoo doll rather than a fair-haired boy. Also, the campaign coincided with America's Bicentennial, and another Walker son was killed, this time by a depth charge that misfired during a waterfront rendition of the *1812 Overture* by the Pompey Pops.

Win recognized the death as a good promotional opportunity, since mourning implies rectitude, so an armada of press trailed after Van when he returned to Vertigo Park for the funeral. They were indecently delighted, though, when Charlotte Haven showed up to pay her respects, too. She had grown tired of the shiny endearments that tinkled like a line of credit from the makeshift Hollywood suitors she'd tolerated since Cliff had vanished. Reading about Van had renewed her pride in him and her own stung idealism, and she wanted to offer her respect to a man she knew respected her. Despite his grief, Van was flourishing and self-confident, since August Dodd Woodhead's was a lame duck candidacy, and people now thronged to Van's blandness as to milk of magnesia after President Torque's chili peppers of deceit. The publicity firm of Scud, Scurry, and Edgewise had convinced even Van of his worthiness, and when he saw Carlotta, he was at his most radiant. Unlike Cliff, he was grateful, lovable, and able to love in return. Win, pragmatic even about his thwarted love, arranged to have Van inspect local blackout emergency supplies by candlelight, and invited Carlotta along. She was entranced by the shrewdly romantic photo opportunity, and Van saw in her, if not his unknown mother, then his childhood, and attributed to her the tantalizing value of everything precious irretrievably lost. Their weaknesses met, orphan to orphan, and he proposed. She accepted, swept on as much by duty to drama as a conviction that this was honorable love.

CHAPTER TEN

WEDDING IN SHADOW

An engaged candidate was a sanguine novelty for the media, especially since the couple was barely thirty and the late president had been long-married as well as grotesque. This would settle any restless speculation about Van's wet-eyed sensitivity, and not only was Carlotta famous, her scar could prove her seriousness even to ambassadors who spoke no English. As Win observed to an aide, she gave good headlines.

The ballyhoo of the election bolstered Carlotta, and she mistook its mood for hers. She reminded herself that she was doing the greatest good she could by joining this good man in his work, but sexual doubt crept in like mice gnawing at the bedboards, and as she lay in a succession of chastely single hotel rooms along the campaign trail, hearing the even, unending inhale of the air conditioner, she wondered if she was making a mistake.

The wedding was scheduled for the weekend before the election. It was pointedly simple, taxpayers take note, held in the basement of Pompey's VFW hall, and instead of gifts the couple requested donations to charity. Carlotta wore a turquoise dress borrowed from the garment workers' union—something new, borrowed, and blue—and for something old, she clutched a bouquet of dead, dried flowers. August Dodd Woodhead's camp tried to compete by having him adopt a Vietnamese baby, but since Win, his real son, was estranged—in fact, he was Van's best man —the heartwarming aspect was overshadowed by the gothic.

As the hired combo played the love theme from *Woman in Jeopardy*, Van's stepfather, Big Bill Walker, approached Carlotta, his red face redder with nuptial wine. "Raise many, many children," he told her, "so no single one will matter too much." Then Chick

Burns, uncomfortable in a borrowed suit, approached and asked Carlotta if she knew where his son was. She honestly didn't, but seeing Cliff's father made a low bell toll in her carillon, and a cold vermouth breathed darkly in her happiness cocktail. Prompted by Chick's questions, she began to imagine she saw Cliff in the shadowy corners of the hall, in soldier's fatigues at the bar with the Secret Service men, behind a pillar or the ziggurat silhouette of the wedding cake. She shivered, feeling that chastised, funky sensation one gets from going too quickly from dazzling sunlight on the beach into a dank, dim changing booth. Van, like the sun, was scrupulous but untouchable. Cliff was the periodically vanishing moon, erotic and preceptor to danger. Her head swam, and not very well.

She faltered from the heat at the crowded reception, but she was brought back to reality, such as it was, by the sudden spectacle of Julienne arriving on the arm of Culvert Booney. Julienne had returned to traditional values, or at least to her childhood address, and set her sights, if not lower, then backwards. She had married Culvert earlier that day. The uselessness of such outdated triumph let Carlotta hope the gesture had nothing to do with her, until Julienne announced she had changed her name once again, this time to Carlotta. Somehow, perhaps numerologically, she hoped to tail Carlotta to the mansion of happiness, to get on some electrified u-dodge-em track to fulfillment. On a night already as fraught with doubt as her wedding was, Carlotta could only faintly murmur congratulations to the couple. She let the mystery of all lives but hers pass around her, and her stepsister receded from her into the unavailing celebrants, glistening into the dark like a desperately polished nickel.

CHAPTER ELEVEN

THE DAWN OF NIGHT

Van won the election, the youngest president in history, with the youngest wife. He chose not only to walk to his inauguration, like a simple man, but to show his trust in the people's voice, he opted to wear a blindfold. The idea was that ordinary citizens would line the streets of Washington that morning and call out directions to him as he advanced, so, through their guidance, he wouldn't run into the curb or take a wrong turn. The gesture was awkward, and for the first time, people noticed his limp, but Carlotta walked by his side throughout, though without touching him, since that would be cheating.

His honeymoon with her, and with the nation, was brief. He did indeed try to make sure everything was right, and in his first hundred days in office mandated sweeping and expensive examinations of military equipment, commercial airlines, hospitals, infant plush toys, traffic-light suspension, escalator speeds, postal sweepstake paper cuts, and all the tangle of conveniences that add up to modern life. The result was safety, but stasis, since air flights, operations, paychecks, and even home delivery of groceries were delayed for days in the Hamlet-slow process of systems analysis. The people, dazed by too much recklessness, now chafed under too much caution. As always, they abhorred lawlessness but decried restriction, and millions wriggled like children confined with allergies they don't believe they have.

Synchronized swimming was added to the roster of Olympic events, with Carlotta as honorary timekeeper, guilty memories of wounding Van assuring her enthusiasm. She declined the many movie offers that poured in, but she did do a series of public service announcements urging Americans not to panic.

Inflation, impatience, and global unrest mounted, and Van's youth now came to be seen as a kind of weakness. He tried to meet with anyone who wanted to, but his schedule became decimated by crackpot retirees, star-struck checkout girls, and bored first graders fulfilling requirements. He came to bed drained but insomniac, and tried to absorb statistical abstracts to make the most of the night. Carlotta had skyrocketed into a sexless marriage.

Eventually, Julienne came to see Carlotta, and seemed contrite and friendly. She even identified herself as Julienne. She was now the honored sister of the First Lady in Vertigo Park, which was still depressed but was selling a few presidential souvenirs. She had her pick of roles at the Pompey Community Playhouse, and sometimes did the weather with Culvert. She was in charge of attaching the Partly Clouded Sun. However, Culvert was weakening, and she looked tired herself. She needed a project. Julienne announced she wanted to write Carlotta's biography, but asked if she might do it in the first person, like a ghostwritten autobiography. Disconcerted by such oblique devotion, and worried by her sister's haggard appearance, Carlotta conceded. She offered to let Julienne come and live with her, but Julienne said it wasn't necessary, that she had the whole book already written in her mind. As she was leaving, Julienne tremblingly asked if Carlotta had any news of Cliff. Carlotta had none, and pity and resentment welled up in her, plus the chilling epiphany that she and Julienne were not so different in this frailty. She shivered as they hugged in parting, and this palpable chip in Carlotta's gilding reassured Julienne that she and her sister were not so different. Julienne left coughing but happier, and Carlotta was shaken to behold herself in one she pitied.

CHAPTER TWELVE

—

DEMANDS IN THE SANDS

Van's pledge of Christian cheek-turning made the Allies nervous, and in no time he was tested pointblank. A busload of reporters covering a movie thriller being filmed in the Middle East was hijacked by terrorists, and they were held hostage in a crudely rigged-up broadcasting studio in the trackless desert hills. Since the reporters and hostages were one, and the terrorists gave them free use of the camera, the coverage was excellent and impassioned, and stressed the crucial importance of their own rescue. The terrorists made no specific demands, but asked that Van make them an offer.

In a messianic spirit, he offered himself, unprotected, in exchange for the reporters. This didn't appeal to the terrorists, though, and they asked for Carlotta instead, since most of them had admired her in the dubbed version of *Blood Pressure*. At first Van wouldn't consider it, but she, eager to do right, convinced him that since he had been willing, she had as much right to self-sacrifice as he did, and it would be vanity in him to forbid her to contribute. After complicated soul-searching, he let her go, "of her own beautiful free will," to the desert to surrender herself. The public, and even the reporters who were thereby released, saw this as spineless and unmanly, to turn over your own wife to terrorists, and a thunderous outcry arose on their return to their customary newsdesks. People pointed out that Van was short for Vanilla, and Vanilla sounded like a girl's name.

Her captors invited Carlotta to become their spokesperson, but before she could negotiate, there was a sudden outbreak of gunfire in the studio, and a group of mercenaries swarmed into the room, and incidentally onto live television. They had spotted the hideaway and, without any idea of its international significance, figured it might have some equipment worth plundering. Once again, her life was saved in a bloody minute, and once again her rescuer was Cliff Burns, the leader of these opportunistic soldiers of fortune. He had hooked up with some survivalists in

Northern California and ended up doing pickup jobs in war-torn areas. Everyone in the studio was killed but Carlotta, and the viewing public never realized she had been spared only by accident.

Van was hounded from office after her return, though it took several weeks for the convulsions to play themselves out. Carlotta stood by her husband, since she believed he had done the right thing, but her stance was unsteady with the reappearance of Cliff, who was posed hugging her by a jubilant press. Cliff had barely known Van in Vertigo Park, but he revived an old schoolyard taunt and teased the president as Van, Van, Born in a Can. A few faint voices pointed out that Cliff hadn't even known Carlotta was in the terrorists' studio, but people admired his sneering good luck. Beyond his own mortification, Van also sensed Carlotta's electric response to Cliff, and, despite her pleas, he resigned and entered a monastery, renouncing worldly things. Haplessly, with his typical waffling, he reappeared a few days later to try to resume his office, an attempted reverse dive the Congress declared inadmissible. Carlotta was torn by Van's torture and her own unresolved passion for Cliff, who had been installed as a guest of the White House by popular demand. Wanting to be strong for Van, trying to avoid encountering Cliff, she nonetheless found herself gasping and dizzy, as if spinning on an amusement park rotary ride, where the floor drops away but one hangs motionless, pinned to the wall by air. She and Van spent a night together weeping as proof of their love, but then he vanished definitively, supposedly to Sri Lanka, though no one was ever quite sure. There were later reports of a blue-eyed penitent there who had taken a vow of silence, and so could not explain himself.

CHAPTER THIRTEEN

———

A WOLF IN DOG'S CLOTHING

Nestor Haze, like the sentimental painters drawn to plagued frontier towns, traveled to Washington to appropriate what seemed an epic tale to him. He offered to write dialog for Cliff during the Senate hearings on the violent rescue of the First Lady. Surprisingly, Cliff accepted, and the two proved well matched. Cliff was the perfect terse loner to speak for blabbermouth, clubby America's wishful image of itself, and Nestor's niblets of corn sounded pithy in Cliff's monotone.

Since Van had trimmed the vice-presidency as needless fat, an immediate election was called for on a write-in basis, out of necessity and as a token of electoral reform; besides, the country was virtually broke. August Dodd Woodhead ran on an I Told You So platform, but this time his son Win decided to run against his father himself, despite the presumption that his acidic manner was unelectable. The family conflict was a sensation, but it made the public tired of Dodd and alienated by Win's witticisms and his tawdry revelations about his childhood spankings. Natural momentum put Cliff in the race, running without any party's support but with the defense that he owed nothing to any machine. His slogan, crafted by Nestor, was Be Proud—He Is. Nestor was also his vice-presidential choice, since Cliff didn't want to meet any strange men in suits and pick one to work with. Also, Shep Woodhead emerged briefly from Lilly Willow, not to endorse his father or his brother, but to reminisce about what good care Cliff had taken of him, and what a good job he'd done running the farm. In Shep's anesthetized mind, it had been a farm.

The public hoped against hope that Cliff and Carlotta would get together romantically, especially since they were high school sweethearts who had dated briefly later. Tabloids urged her to hear his plea, though as always he seemed to desire her without any particular neediness. She resolved to resist him, and announced she could not keep falling under his spell, only to be abandoned. He grinned and shrugged.

The next day Cliff called a press conference and announced he was marrying Carlotta, that her husband had been declared not only dead but already dead for several years, so she was free to wed without criticism. Carlotta was half thrilled and half affronted, since although this was her dream come true, he hadn't asked her first. The country went wild for it, and as it had been with Van, the luster of others' approval burnished Cliff to a husbandly hue. Besides, he seemed to be civilizing his Dodge City heart, thanks to Nestor's gulch-brown banalities and his own taste for authority. Anyway, she reasoned, the system of checks and balances would keep him, if not in line, then at least on hand. They were married in the Rose Garden, and Cliff wore a suit. Julienne was invited to the wedding, but she claimed she had already written the chapter about it, and the trip would be superfluous.

CHAPTER FOURTEEN

———

OUR LADY OF THE TAILSPIN

Cliff won the election, and drove himself to his inauguration in a specially customized limousine, cutting more than a half hour off the ceremony's previous record for speed. He raced the engine noisily whenever the motorcade was forced to pause along the way, and startled dignitaries when he slid across the polished floor on his stomach during the gala ball. Yes, Cliff was young, but not, everyone emphasized, as young as Van Walker had been. Win Woodhead had disappeared forever right after his defeat, either to seek out Van or to sulk without end, but August Dodd Woodhead came to the inauguration, to show that at his advanced age he no longer minded anything.

Once in office, Cliff froze wages and encouraged the barter system whenever possible, since objects themselves were incapable of inflation. He made his father Secretary of Transportation, and they decreed hundreds of miles of highways to be public drag strips. He relished setting the limited fires his Secretary of the Interior suggested for the national parks' sake, and he ordained frequent jet defense drills that shattered windows with sonic booms. He announced that prosecuting drug users was too costly, and as he had with Shep, declared that everyone who wanted to use drugs could do so, only now in a special reservation fashioned from the state of Oregon, a sort of national Smoking Section. He was a champion of deregulation, and gave heavy tax breaks to American auto manufacturers, but he seemed sullen and mistrustful whenever he had to speak to foreigners, even the English. His tough position on American defense provoked some killings of Americans in Europe, but he responded by recalling all Americans, civilian or military, from overseas. This "Americans in America" policy wreaked havoc with international business, not to mention international marriages, but as terrorism discouraged travel, and protectionism made importing and exporting complicated, slowly a gargantuan medieval insularity developed.

True to his *Manolog* days, the new chief executive also liked dropping out of sight for days at a time, which thrilled people only at first, and his animal freedom started to seem as dangerous as Van's angelic weakness. Although Nestor wrote speeches for him including allusions to family and sharing, Cliff seemed gruff and distracted, and Carlotta felt no closer to him than she had in California. He was growing away from her without ever quite being hers. He may have felt it would be weak to rely on her, sympathetic as she was, but whenever he disappeared, it was she who had to put on a brave face for the press while they wondered if there were other women or just a secret hideout.

To complicate the national paranoia, a sexually transmitted illness began to ravage the population. It was eventually discovered to have begun in the lamb-skin condoms prescribed in Van Walker's administration to curb venereal disease. Apparently the lambs had been grazed on radioactive former bomb test-site prairies, and the mutant virus they acquired was hard to shake. People immediately stopped using condoms, but it was already too late. Fatal Urogenital Carnal Kinesis claimed its victims without any right to such claims, and often drove them mad first. Even Nestor, who had been careful to protect himself in his dalliances with Mexican girls, went from merely garrulous to incomprehensible, and his last words were something about the Wagon Train heading ever westward to the Milky Way.

So, not only travel but socializing was curtailed, with television as the safe alternative, and this was where Carlotta entered her truly legendary phase. Under the supervision of the secretaries of State and of Health, she made numerous cheerful videos in which she seemed not only to have a nice romantic date with the viewer, she went on simulated vacations to Europe, bought attractive furniture, went to friendly parties, and even raised several pleasant and appreciative children. She herself was childless, and the husband in her videos went unseen, but millions were grateful for the apparently fulfilled life they vicariously experienced from her tapes. Her greatest seller was a video in which she lived in a peaceful small town called Verdant Park, and everyone in it had a sweetheart and a job. People now referred to her as Our Carlotta, since it was hip to know her real name, and besides, it was more comforting than Charlotte.

CHAPTER FIFTEEN

DARING DAYLIGHT DESTINY

Julienne appeared at the White House late one afternoon, sunken-eyed and weirdly dressed for a formal ball, with a huge handwritten manuscript that she wheeled in unwrapped on a dolly. When Carlotta came to her, Julienne confided too loudly that Culvert had committed suicide the day before. Depressed by his sickness, for starters, he had thrown himself from the highest finial of his father's unfinished folly, Vertigo Park, the haunted palace of storm windows. Julienne had then decided she was finished with her biography and headed for Washington. It was called *Carlotta Made*, and she presented it to her sister with shaking hands. It bore no relation to reality, however, beyond its vaguely pornographic title, and though illegible, would have read more like a hack's misremembrance of the Book of Revelation than like Carlotta's actual rags-to-riches story. It seemed to presume that Carlotta, sometimes called Charlotte, was the cause of the sunrise and of springtime, of snowfall and rebirth. The text dwelled on a serpent called Horizon, and had no clear-cut beginning or ending, since the pages were unnumbered and Julienne seemed unconcerned about those pages that blew away when she moved the dolly from place to place. She announced that she was Carlotta, that Cliff was her husband, and that they were going away together forever.

Carlotta was anxious, but invited Julienne to rest there for the night. Julienne spent it sleeplessly calling out her own name, which was difficult to call a good sign. Cliff, who was in residence at the time, and Carlotta could hear her cries even from their room, and though Cliff dismissed Julienne as self-chopped mincemeat, he was shaken, and for the first time in his experience, was sexually impotent. Carlotta was sympathetic, from which he recoiled, because it made him feel weak. She secretly hoped that this, his first unluckiness, might be a breakthrough to fuller humanity for him.

Julienne came to breakfast late, still in her formal dress, and declared that her name was now Fury, which she hoped didn't sound too much like a horse. She then produced a small handgun, which Cliff had insisted be provided in every guest bedroom, and rushed into the Rose Garden, where he was negotiating with Romulus and Remus Portonovo, the wealthy Italian realtors, for the sale of Rome as a movable theme park. She shot Cliff in the heart, and then herself, warning the Italians they would be next. Apparently she had been driven mad not just from jealousy but from the Fatal Urogenital Carnal Kinesis that had incubated in her since her performance in *Will Wanda Never Cease?*

Aides screamed, and Romulus and Remus wailed Latinate expressions of horror. Carlotta rushed to cradle the dying Cliff, who shuddered with surprise. He had never felt pain before. He faintly joked that once the dick goes, so do the reflexes, and with his index finger tenderly, for once, tracing the scar on her cheek, he expired. Carlotta stiffened with confusion, and at this moment Shep Woodhead appeared, fresh out of Lilly Willow, and asked if there were any job openings.

E P I L O G

As dazed as grieved, Carlotta and her attendant Congress tried to figure out what to do. Cliff had not named another vice-president after Nestor's death, claiming it would be defeatist, and the public had lost its will to endorse anyone. August Woodhead offered to supervise business matters for the interim, and no one had the self-possession to object very strenuously. Carlotta's old public service messages discouraging panic were brought out and aired again, and since she was identified only as Our First Lady, no updating was required. Now she was the public's only symbol of continuity, or grace, or for that matter, survival, even if she didn't understand or feel it herself. Her classmates, Culvert, her driving teacher, Van, Nestor, moviegoers, the terrorists, Julienne, and now the world had seen her as a necessary figure of salvation, her blood-red hair absorbing their sorrows. Cliff alone had never seen her symbolically, but as a fellow creature. He didn't know her either, but he took her directly, which was his power over her. Now she was truly alone, unwitnessed though universally watched, a living effigy of an unliving thing, a shipwrecked tourist finally too exhausted to go on denying her divinity to insistent natives.

Without intending to, she was carried like a standard beyond her own battlefield of good and evil, into a mood historians call postmodernity and psychologists call middle age. She was, in time, swept beyond the polar griefs of Van and Cliff. A peaceful, almost embalming fluid of fatalism cooled her veins, and the world saw it as stateliness. Once he acceded to the presidency after his father's death, Shep offered to be her consort, but Carlotta needed to be properly magnetized.

After thesis and antithesis, she drifted not so much to a synthesis as to a tertiary finale. She became the mistress of the Portonovo twins, who had loved her as the Madonna from the moment they saw her hold her dying husband. They set up a rococo villa for her on the Mediterranean, and shared her unpossessively, for theirs was a Siamese ambition. She herself didn't trouble to tell them apart, and they were simply identified internationally—insofar as that was possible with deteriorating communications—as the Brothers Who Sold Rome. They had acquired all the real estate in the Eternal City, incidentally obliging them to buy the Catholic church itself, to dismantle and ship its ruins and architectural beauties worldwide as accessible local tourist attractions, since terrorism had virtually ended recreational travel. Technically, they were the Pope, and they authorized the subdivision of cathedrals everywhere into prestige co-op apartments. Carlotta acquiesced to them without loving them, a sort of heart's retirement. The villa was perpetually obscured to waking eyes by the sun on the sea, and she could distract herself with the art objects Romulus and Remus pilfered from their own museums for her. They were certainly doting and undemanding, and any shouting they did was over the phone to their construction—or rather, deconstruction—crews.

When word came from the last surviving Walker son that the shell of Vertigo Park had finally collapsed, Carlotta was stirred by an unexpected pang of nostalgia. Sensing her wistfulness, the twins had Sacajawea High School brought over and reassembled for her on a hillside near the villa. She toured it with an enigmatic smile, as befitted an icon, pausing occasionally but finding no consolation in its familiarity. Her life's plot eluded her, but when she sat to reflect in the cavernous old auditorium, she seemed to identify something in the now peeling mural of Sacajawea, Lewis and Clark's young Indian guide, at their journey's end.

The mural stretched high across the front wall of the room, above the twin masks of Comedy and Tragedy that hung over the stage where so many hopeful diplomas had been distributed. Sacajawea stood on a gilded beach with the two explorers, bathed in a sunset that leapt as close as a bonfire, and she superfluously pointed out the limitless ocean before her. The two men were in darkness behind her, as if she were real and they were her halves in shadow. She seemed to be Lewis and Clark's intercessor with nature, yet surprised by it herself, painted into a moment of perpetual and foregone discovery, the inlander awed at her first and continuous look at the Pacific Ocean.

Carlotta breathed deep, and closed her eyes.

THE SOLAR YEARBOOK

MERCURY	VENUS	EARTH

Small, dark, and speedy . . . "Race you round the furnace!" . . . No moon and doesn't want one . . . Daredevil or homebody? . . . Party trick: fries eggs and freezes ice cubes at the same time.

Track 3, 4; First Place, World Series.

Mysterious, or thinks she is . . . "Welcome to our mist!" . . . Really bright, but looks aren't everything . . . I C CO_2! . . . Cute, but that cloud cover . . . Her oceans were notions . . . Who's minding the hothouse?

Morning Star; Evening Star.

Cootie-catcher . . . Wet and wild . . . Talk, talk, talk . . . Oh those baby-blues . . . Air to spare, but smokes too much . . . Thinks the sun revolves around *her*.

History 1, 2, 3, 4; Art; Choir; R.O.T.C.; Most Populous.

	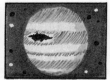	
MARS	**JUPITER**	**SATURN**

Always blushing . . . Long time no sea . . . Eerie canals . . . Premature polar caps . . . Ever consider moisturizer? . . . Sick of little-green-men jokes . . . "Two Moons Have I" . . . and one is nuts.

Most Likely to Have Had Life.

Big Joe . . . Bold and cold, with a tight hold . . . *How many moons???* . . . Don't mention that big red spot . . . B.M.O.C. . . . Loads of ammonia, but nothing to wash . . . Slept through Remedial Atmosphere . . . Orbit: anywhere he wants.

Gravity (Captain); Biggest.

Beat the dress code . . . Showoff at hula hoop . . . Brrrrrr-illiant . . . Hope you like methane . . . Class clown, but don't tell her.

Best Dressed; Biggest (Runner-Up); Most Moons; 1000-M.P.H. Winds.

URANUS	**NEPTUNE**	**PLUTO**
"C'mon, guys, it's pronounced *'You're a niss'* " . . . And he is . . . Green mien, clean scene . . . quiet, wisely . . . Hydrogen fiend . . . A five-moon man . . . "See you next century!" *Metal Shop; Most Average.*	"Which one are you again?" . . . Not exactly molten . . . Far out, but only technically . . . Never volunteers . . . Solid . . . "No, it's Uranus that has the five moons!" *Ice Show; Outer Solar System Monitor.*	Loner type . . . Recent transfer . . . Easy to miss . . . Small as a moon, but those long midnight joyrides . . . No curfew . . . "My folks say he is bad, but I know he is sad." *Strangest Orbit; Most Days Absent.*

MARRED BLISS

The front porch of **JANE**'s *family home.* **JANE** *arranges roses in a vase.* **DINK** *sits on the glider, reading the paper or just enjoying the evening. A typical midwestern scene.* **JANE** *is a pretty, prissy, inhibited young woman, wearing starched, modest clothes.* **DINK** *is a regular lug who's been talked into marriage but is willing to turn himself over to it.*

JANE: Darkling?

DINK *(looking up from his paper)***:** What is it, dulling?

JANE: I thought we'd have ruses for the centerpieces. For us, and for all the guest tables. Ruses *are* traditional.

DINK: Ruses it is. *(He continues reading.)*

JANE *(after a restless pause)*: Oh, honey, just *sink*!

DINK: What do you want me to sink about?

JANE: In less than forty-eight horrors, you and I will be moan and woof! *(Grins.)* Isn't it amassing?

DINK: It *is* amassing! *(He lowers his paper thoughtfully.)* So much has harpooned in just a few thief years!

JANE: It steams like only yesterday that you were the noise next door.

DINK: And you were that feckless-faced cod sitting up in the old ache tree!

JANE: And now we're encaged! I can hardly wait till we're marred!

DINK: Oh, hiney! *(He rises and makes to enfold her in his arms.)*

JANE: Now, now! I'm sure the tame will pass quickly till our hiney-moon! *(She eases out of his grasp.)* I'll go get you some of that nice saltpeter taffy that Smother brought back from A Frantic City.

*(**JEERY**, a sexy, slouching sailor, appears at one corner of the stage.)*

JEERY: Hello? . . . Any him at home? *(He carries a tiny bouquet.)*

JANE: Oh, my gash! It's Jeery, my old toyfriend!

DINK: Jeery! That bump! What's *he* brewing here?

JANE: Oh, dueling! Try to control your tamper! I'm sure he means no charm! Don't do anything you might regress!

*(**JEERY** approaches.)*

JEERY: Hollow!—Revised to see me?

JANE: Hollow, Jeery.

DINK: Hollow.

(Pause.)

JEERY: I'm completely beware that I'm out of police here. But *(looks to* **JANE***)*—for old climb's sake, Jane, I brought you this little bunch of foul airs. A token of my excess steam. Lots of lack to you. And much lack to you, too, Dink.

JANE *(unsure)*: Wail . . . *(She decides to accept the flowers.)* Spank you, Jeery.

DINK: Spank you very much.

JEERY: My shaft is at rancor in the harbor, and they gave me whore leave. I heard you were engorged, and I just wanted to slop by and pave my regrets.

JANE *(uncomfortably)*: Well, blank you!

DINK: Blank you very much.

JANE *(uneasy with this standoff)*: I think you two have already messed, haven't you?

JEERY: Oh, we've thrown each other for years!

DINK: We went to the same cruel . . . till Jeery dripped out to join the Nervy.

JANE: Of course, I remainder all that now! *(She is eager to lessen the awkwardness.)* Um—do you haunt to sit down?

JEERY: Well, only for a menace. *(They all sit down on the glider.)* I'm hooded over to Pain Street. There's a big trance at the Social Tub. I'll probably go and chick it out. *(There is an awkward silence as they sit on the crowded glider.)* Wail, wail, wail . . . So when do you two tie the net?

JANE: The day after temerity!

JEERY: That soon?

DINK *(curtly)*: We've been enraged for over a year.

JEERY: Well, concatenations!

DINK: Rank you very much. *(Tense pause.)* . . . Jeery, it's getting awfully lout! You don't want to miss the trance!

*(From the other entrance comes **ALAS**, a provocatively dressed woman with elaborate hair and a loose manner.)*

ALAS: Hell's own? Hell's own?

JANE *(aside)*: Oh, no! Is that who I slink it is? Why won't she let us align?

*(**ALAS** advances.)*

ALAS: Hell's own, every burden! Hell's own, Dink! . . .

DINK *(uncomfortable but heated)*: Hell's own, Alas! . . . Fantasy seething you here!

JANE *(tartly)*: I thought you'd be at the Social Tub trance, Alas. Aren't you on the degradation committee?

ALAS *(offering a gift-wrapped bottle)*: I may stoop by there later. I sinfully wanted to winch you both all the beast. Let icons be icons. Here's a battle of damn pain for you. I hype you enjoy it.

JANE *(suspicious)*: How sweat of you. *(She takes the bottle and puts it aside.)* You know Jeery, don't you, Alas?

ALAS: Yes, we mated years ago. How's the Nervy, Jeery?

JEERY: Great! I was born to be a soiler.

(There is another awkward silence as they regard her.)

DINK *(to* **ALAS***)*: Um—would you like to hit with us, Alas? Jane, you don't grind if Alas hits with us, do you?

JANE: Well, the glider's getting awfully clouded!

ALAS: I'll just loin against the railing! *(She poses against the pillar seductively.)*

DINK: No, here, have my seed! *(He stands.)*

JANE: Dallying! *(She pulls him back into his seat.)* I think she'd rather remain stunning!

DINK *(getting agitated)*: Jeery, you could awful her *your* seat! Don't they teach you manners in the harmed surfaces? (**JEERY** *bristles.)*

JANE *(to avoid a scene)*: Look, qualm down! Maybe we should admit this is an awkward saturation! I have complete face in you, Dink, but I think it's in power taste for your old street-part to come around so soon before our welding!

ALAS *(offended)*: I can't bereave this! There's no reason to be subspecies, Jane!

JANE *(affronted)*: No?

ALAS: This is a good-wall visit, that's all! You're just high-stung!

DINK *(chiming in his objections)*: And what about Jeery here! I don't luck having him luring at you!

JEERY *(contemptuously)*: Oh, relapse, Dink! Afraid she'll realize her must-ache before the sorrow-money? *(to* **ALAS***:)* He's in debt, it's a mortgage of convenience!

JANE *(frightened by this sudden passion)*: Toys, please! Clam yourself! *(Earnestly, to* **DINK***:)* Dink, don't drought yourself this way! Where's the strong, stabled man I'm taking to be altered? You know I lug you, I'll always lug you. *(She puts her arms around him ma-*

ternally.) I want ours to be a beautiful cremation-trip. But it has to be based on *truss. (She hugs him even more suffocatingly, and not erotically.)* I want to be able to *truss* you.

DINK *(too independently to suit **JANE**)*: All I did was offer Alas my seed. You act like I rammed off with her!

JANE *(feeling dressed down before company)*: Well, maybe you'd rather ram off with her! She's been trying to reduce you since she got here!

ALAS *(angry)*: Don't spike like that to me! I bitter go.

JANE *(her insecurity making her hysterical)*: Stew where you are! You're the claws of this! You *slot*!

ALAS *(sneering at **JANE**)*: What a little squirrel! I have nothing but potty for you!

(The women suddenly slap each other; the men must intervene.)

JEERY *(restraining **ALAS**)*: The whole tissue is ridiculous! Fighting over a man who's in doubt up to his ears!

DINK: At least I'm not diddled with funereal disease, you bellow-jellied bullbottomed sin of the beach!

JEERY: You sod-damned cowbird!

(The men fight; now the women must intervene.)

ALAS: Stomp it! Stomp it this minute!

(There is a momentary silence, as they all recover from their wounds.)

JANE: Why are we having such trouble trying to communicate?

DINK *(taking the lead)*: Look. Alas . . . I heave nothing but harpy memories of our time together. I depreciate your good winces, but Jane and I are to be marred, and that's that. *(He looks to* **JANE** *to match his definitive renunciation.)*

JANE *(taking* **JEERY**'s *hand briefly)*: And . . . Jeery . . . I leave you very much. You know that. But that's all winter under the fridge. *(She turns to* **ALAS**.*)* Alas, I'm sorry I lost my torpor.

ALAS *(with dignity)*: I understand. And I axe-up your apology. Anyway, for your inflammation, I'm getting marred myself. To Henry Silverstone.

JANE *(impressed)*: The banker! But he's rather old for you, isn't he?

ALAS: Luckily, he's in very good wealth. *(A car horn honks from offstage.)* There's my chauffeured limbo now. I'd better get gilding. Conglomerations, and gall the best! . . . Goad bye!

DINK *(feeling bested)*: Bile!

JANE *(feeling outdone)*: Bile!

*(***ALAS*** exits.* ***JEERY*** *now feels superfluous.)*

JEERY: Her own limbo! . . . Well, I guess I should leave you two lifeboats alone!

JANE: Thanks for the foul airs, Jeery! Enjoy the trance!

JEERY: Maybe I'll meet *my* future broad!

DINK *(as if to a buddy)*: That's the right platitude!

JEERY: So long! Have a lot of skids!

DINK: Bile!

JANE: Bile! *(***JEERY*** goes.)* He's a good spore, isn't he?

DINK *(reluctantly)*: I gas so.

JANE *(hugging him consolingly)*: But you're the uphill of my eye!

DINK: Oh, hiney! *(He holds and tries to kiss her, but she resists him.)* Oh, come on! Ploys? Pretty ploys?

(She relents and gives him a peck and then quickly raises **ALAS***'s gift bottle between them.)*

JANE: Oh, look! A vintage battle of damn pain! Let's celibate! *(She pops it open and pours some of it into two empty lemonade glasses on the porch table. She raises her glass.)* Here, let's test each other! *(They toast.)* To *ice*! **DINK:** To *ass*!

(They drink.)

JANE: Oh, galling! Our life together is going to be *blitz*!

(Blackout.)

A TALL TALE

America's privately owned, fertilizer-enriched soil
has nurtured some mighty big men—legends like
Slipp'ry Joe Hartford, who actually sold Mother Nature unemployment insurance, or Lightnin' Lefko-
witz, the Wall Street Flash, who traded bonds so fast
that no one could tell if they were really there or not.
And every boy in B school has heard the story of
Loophole Sam, who got out of both death *and* taxes.
Yes, the doings and boastings of these tall-in-the-
portfolio characters have filled many an annual report, but none of them has ever been bigger or more
diversified than a horizon-blocking butte of a booster
they call Johnny Business, and if the busboys have

finished clearing the tables, lend an ear to the story I've been so well paid to tell. Lights, please?

Johnny was only the biggest man that ever gripped a boardroom table, and that includes your ex-football players in public relations. Why, when he was born, he was fifteen stories high, with a view of the park on two sides! His pa was a profiteering man with an automobile so long, it started pulling into the hospital driveway the morning Johnny was born, and to this day it hasn't completely arrived. Johnny's mother was the infamous Ma Bell, a broad-shouldered woman who could hear a million conversations at once, and still not change her mind.

One day when he was three, she took him out to lunch and said to him. "Son—you gonna be a deal-drivin' man, like yo' daddy?" And Johnny—through a representative—answered, "I have no problem with that."

When Johnny Business was a little baby
Sittin' on his Mammy's knee,
He said, "Government restrictions on my right to
    make a profit
Gonna be the death of me, Lord, Lord,
Gonna be the death of me."

Well, it wasn't long before Johnny's pa was reduced to nothing by revenooers, and his poor old Ma got divested, so Johnny quit Junior Achievement and headed out on his own. Next slide, please. He made himself an attaché case out of an old airplane hangar, and along with his trusty secretary, Babe the Blue Blood, headed south.

"South, Babe!" he told her, and held on high a billfold the size of a billboard. "South—to the Sunbelt!"

Johnny Business went to the Sunbelt,
He rented a penthouse there—
It was up so high, he looked down on the sky,
And he had to pay extra for the air, Lord, Lord,
He had to pay extra for the air!

Johnny was such a fast talker, he could sell feathers to a fish, retail, and in no time he cast a long shadow from Dallas to Atlanta. Old Babe had to do a mountain of Xeroxing as high as the Wrigley Building every morning before breakfast, and what they didn't want kept they used for landfill to build high rises on. He had more credit cards than there are things to buy, and he worked it so he could charge the new ones on the old ones, and the old ones on the new ones, and not even your auditor could have figured out who was due what. And when Johnny took a client out to lunch, he drank his martinis out of old water towers from bankrupt railroads. "Here's how!" he'd laugh. "Happy hour is here to stay!"

Of course, people always get jealous when you're big and jolly. Some sunken-eyed baloney-for-lunch types tried to get Johnny tied down, though of course they were too cash-scrawny to take him on in any leveraged way. No, they had to tattle, like a runt to a playground monitor. What happened was, one day Johnny was visiting a mining operation he was thinking of selling, and when he lay on his belly and squinted down that shaft, he didn't like what he wasn't seeing.

"It's Monday, Frank," he told his foreman. "Where are all the miners?"

Frank took to trembling so his clipboard started to splinter. "They ain't workin', Johnny!" he stammered. "Some kind of itty bitty scraggly ol' foreign birdy told 'em to go out on strike for safer conditions!"

Johnny's scorn fell like acid rain on alkaline earth. "Nothin' in life is safe!" he roared. "America didn't get built on safety! Gimme that shovel, Frank, I'll do the mining myself!"

Johnny took hold of a gigantic shovel and was about to be labor and capital both at once, when suddenly, three little tiny woman lawyers you could barely see came up behind him and hit him with a Cease and Desist whammy. The first one had once got Christmas tabled till Easter, and the second one had taken over Hell until the Devil could refinance. The tiniest of the three was also the meanest. She was from the IRS, and was so good at tax collecting she could find pockets on a shadow. The three of them together carried a roll of red tape so thick a man couldn't even think of home without a dozen feasibility studies first.

Of course, Johnny's back was broader than those little woman lawyers were motivated to wrestle, since they worked on salary only, and he threw them faster than rodeo clowns off a bronco. Then he went ahead and dug into that mine until it plumb collapsed from happiness, and to this day they call the hole he left the Grand Canyon, in honor of the thousand dollars he paid himself to do it. Then for dessert he cut down all the forest in those parts, slicker than a ballplayer shaving on a TV commercial. And without those pesky regulators, Johnny started growing and growing and *growing*—right in front of the media, so ask them if you don't believe me—and pretty soon it took three strong men just to *conceive* of how rich he was!

Finally, right when Johnny was so big he was actually twice as large as himself, there was a market-rattling explosion that made analysts bark as far away as Tacoma, and when the hype had cleared, there wasn't anything left in Johnny Business's shoes but the air rights.

He was true to his code, even if he did explode—
And you have to give him credit, yes you do, Lord, Lord,
You have to give him credit, yes you do . . .

Where did he get to? Oh, some say he went and jumped out a window, but you and I both know there's not enough distance on this earth for a man that big to fall far enough to hurt himself. Others say he died from a heart attack after all that hard work he should have been delegating, and still others have the gold-plated brass to say they've seen his carcass on display at Neiman Marcus—but after all the bespectacled Sunday morning commentary floats off into what no one watched yesterday, the real question is, Do dreams like Johnny's ever really die? Sometimes, on an autumn evening, when trading has been particularly heavy, give a listen to the wind. Maybe you'll hear a distant voice saying, " . . . *I'll get back to you!*"

That'll be Johnny.

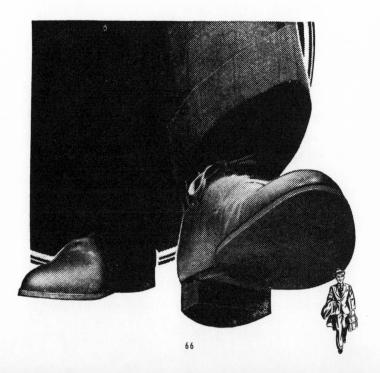

QUESTIONS FOR REVIEW

1. Where is the story set? Do you think having a setting adds to the story? Where are you set? Defend your answer.

2. Dinah repeatedly complains about the darkness at Seven Birches. Is it really darkness? What does she really mean? Think of examples from real life of someone saying things you can barely understand to show everyone how unhappy and alone they are. Make a list.

3. Who survives the fire Dinah sets, and why? Who flees into the night? What happens to Wobbles? (Hint: *Grrrrrr.*)

4. Of the three kinds of conflict—Man versus Man, Man versus Nature, and Man versus Himself—which kinds are in evidence here? (Example: When Doctor Luger's eugenically bred killer ants attack his experimental Ape Maiden, it counts as both Man versus Nature and Man versus Himself—and, arguably, Nature versus Nature.)

5. When Squiffy decides to kick Lars, some-

thing unexpected follows. What? Go kick someone larger than yourself and describe what follows. Be specific.

6. What famous character does Brannigan resemble? Consider his miraculous powers at Dinah's poorly planned party, his death in Crossville, and his surprising resuscitation at Doctor Easter's clinic. Defend your answer.

7. Discuss the perfectly good reasons someone might have for shooting another person, especially in the unorthodox way Dinah shoots Lars. Make a list of people who are bucking for just such treatment. You may include world figures as well as family members and friends.

8. What is it with Dinah? Be specific.

9. Stories consist of rising action, climax, and denouement. Is this true of life? Why or why not? Is it true of New Year's Eve? Why or why not?

10. If this story were a pie, what flavor would it be? If it were a pie that happened to be able to speak, what kind of story would that pie be likely to tell? Would it be this story? If it were a pie that could talk but something was terribly wrong, maybe something psychosomatic or a scandal in its past, and it just didn't, or wouldn't, talk, what kind of thing might be done to that pie to encourage it or even force it to talk? Think before answering.

EXTRA CREDIT PROJECT: Defend yourself.

THE CORPSE HAD FRECKLES

The summer air hung as heavy and still as a significant pause in a personal hygiene lecture. Overhead, the desert sun glared down like a censorious, fire-lashed cyclopean eye on tourist and tarantula alike. Inside the thick adobe walls of Rancho Contento, however, all was so cool and dim that tomatoes wouldn't even ripen. Bitty Borax and her legitimate cousin Anodyne sat in their grandfather's well-dusted library of old deeds and desert realty law books, chatting away the afternoon. Ice cubes made the milk in their glasses even colder than regular cold milk, and their own mild dispositions contrasted with the scorching day outside.

"Mmmm," Bitty murmured, idly fiddling with the tiny cattle-skull motif that capped her swizzle stick. "It looks hot enough out there to roast a ghost!" Ordinarily, Bitty was as pert and direct as a prize show terrier, only with straight hair, but the languorous pace of her desert vacation had relaxed the young crime-solver to the point of whimsy.

"Could you really roast a ghost?" Anodyne wondered aloud, and tried to sip her milk through her swizzle stick, forgetting for a moment that it wasn't a straw. Anodyne wasn't the brightest light on the Christmas tree, but she was always glad to be brought down out of the attic.

"I don't know, Anodyne," reflected Bitty. "It's metaphysical, isn't it? There was that time in the Hindi fanatics' tomb when I set what I thought was a ghost afire, but it was just a thuggee soapnapper in a bedsheet."

"Yes, I got your postcard," Anodyne remembered. "I didn't think you were going to make it!"

"Well, that's all lemonade under the bridgework now," Bitty countered breezily. "Let's dwell on the utter safety of this moment."

"All right," said Anodyne sportingly. "I'm thinking of going sunbathing in the gulch. Would you like to join me?"

"No, thanks," Bitty smiled. "I'm too high-spirited to sunbathe. I would never lie down if it weren't to go right to sleep. And anyway, Aunt Addle should be back soon from gathering stalagmites for luncheon centerpieces down at the old cavern. She may need help cleaning herself up. I know the radiation level there is next to nothing, but she'll want to be decontaminated—just for ritual's sake."

"Poor Aunt Addle," Anodyne mused. "She's been so restless since Uncle Fleck disappeared." Aunt Addle was neither of their mothers, but the Boraxes were a close extended family.

Suddenly, the sound of careening flesh knocking knickknacks off pedestals resounded from the ranch's vestibule. The two girls leapt to their feet as if in reflexive response to an unholy but irresistible national anthem.

"Prairie dogs on loco weed!" guessed Anodyne, edgily snapping her swizzle stick in two.

"Maybe it's the surly half-breed gardener getting the jump on happy hour!" Bitty postulated speedily. "But we'll never know if we don't go look!"

They rushed to the vestibule. There stood Aunt Addle, shaking like a guilty verdict held by a jury foreman afraid to read it. Bits of cat fur clung to her hair and apron, and if she had gathered any stalagmites, she was empty-handed now.

"Aunt Addle!" Bitty raced to her. "What's wrong? Did you just discover the key to a very old and dangerous secret?"

Aunt Addle was as unhinged as a screen door in a twister, and stared at the girls as if she had just awakened into an intense and unconvincing fiction. "The—! The—!" she began, and fell senseless to the floor.

"Gee, that's not much to go on," said Bitty gravely. "So many things begin with 'the.'" She knelt to examine her unkempt relation.

"There may not be anything to worry about," offered Anodyne faintly. "She does this every night, and sometimes she doesn't get up till morning."

"Yes, but this is early afternoon," Bitty pointed out sternly. "Aunt Addle wouldn't abuse her only house-dress this way." She felt for a pulse, and her own face paled to a cleanser-colored white. "I—I'm sorry, Anodyne," she announced finally. "Aunt Addle is . . . unconscious!"

Anodyne's eyes widened, twin burnt cookies of terror. "Unconscious! What does that mean?" Again, Anodyne tended to be a few measures behind the rest of the band.

"Unconscious is like being asleep—and not even knowing it!" Bitty explained. Silence fell over them like a dust cover.

Then, just as suddenly, they were interrupted by an ominous clicking sound from the porch. "Bitty!" breathed Anodyne. "Someone—or some*thing*—is on the front porch! This is scary times six!"

Bitty opened the thick windowless wooden door. There stood a handsome young man in a pristine lab coat, scanning the mission furniture with a Geiger counter.

"I'm sorry if I startled you," he smiled. "I was driving by and noticed a gum wrapper on your porch. I took the liberty of putting it in your trash can, but I thought I should check your radiation levels while I was at it. I hope you don't mind. I'm Blaine Salvage."

Anodyne sighed with relief. "Of course, Doctor Salvage! Bitty, Doctor Salvage is in the teen-surgery ward at Las Perdidas Hospital. He helped me out with that little problem of mine in *The Mystery of the Co-Ed Dormitory*. This is my cousin, Bitty Borax. She was the one who saved the governor's dog from those blackmailers."

"I certainly read about that, Miss Borax," the doctor grinned. "You're beautifully groomed. Will you marry me?"

Bitty tastefully deflected his question. "Nice to meet you, Doctor." A pause followed through which a symbolic train could have been driven.

"I'll see to this old lady," Doctor Salvage offered. "She's dead, I take it?" He stepped inside.

"Oh, no, just unconscious, thanks!" Bitty answered.

The doctor lifted Aunt Addle into his arms and carried her out of the room. "I'll just take her into the kitchen. If you like, I can perform an autopsy. Can I fix either of you a sandwich while I'm in there?"

"No thanks!" Bitty replied. "I never eat. But you might make one for Anodyne—she's supposed to stay fifteen pounds heavier than me at all times. But again, Doctor, Aunt Addle isn't dead."

"I'm surprised," he called from the kitchen. "She got her hands awfully dirty at the old cavern!"

"Isn't he strong?" chirped Anodyne secretively. "He must lift a lot of heavy syringes!"

Bitty was preoccupied, however. "How did he know Aunt Addle was at the old cavern?"

"Well, maybe he's a sleuth like you, and knows all the acid sludge in these parts by type."

Before they could resolve their curiosity, though, a sound of lumbering footsteps echoed from the cellar, ghostly clunks ascending the steps to the vestibule. With a disdainful clatter, a large, sinister man in a frayed dressing gown appeared, carrying several old-looking hatboxes.

"Mister Packaday, you startled us!" gasped Anodyne. "We thought you'd be in town at the Carnal Nugget, getting inspiration."

Pilsener Packaday was a houseguest of the Borax family, a dissolute but assured writer from the East who had once saved Uncle Fleck in a beanery collapse. He was supposedly on a writer's retreat, but several times Bitty had seen him furtively descend to the wine cellar when he said he was going out to scan the horizon charismatically.

"How's your new book coming?" she asked cautiously, watching the disheveled celebrity place the hatboxes on a side table.

"I mustn't be disturbed," he answered testily, and lit a cigarette. He proceeded to stack and rearrange the inscrutable boxes as if absorbed in a game whose rules were private and unfathomable. "Leave me, please. I'm very busy."

"I hope all this commotion hasn't broken your concentration," Bitty ventured. "Aunt Addle had a fit of some kind."

Mister Packaday turned to her indifferently, his eyes as cold as fancy spherical ice cubes one gets from novelty ice cube trays. "I heard nothing. I must work. I tire of you both. Go at once."

This seemed a presumptuous request in a family room, but Bitty bore in mind that he was a guest. "Have you made any progress on your *Quick Weight-Loss Way to Riches*, Mister Packaday?" He continued to move the hatboxes around the table, as if seeking a perfect configuration.

Anodyne attempted to flatter him into responding. "A famous writer like you must know a lot about human suffering," she offered hopefully.

"It's true, I do. Get out please."

Bitty felt she had to be frank. "Isn't there enough privacy in the room we fixed up for you, Mister Packaday?"

He eyed her as if by legal compulsion, and the ash from his cigarette fell to the floor like a whispered insult. "I can't work with a dead body lying around. Tell whoever changes the linen."

Anodyne was becoming agitated, a sign that she was finally growing up. "A dead body! Whose could it be? It doesn't seem to be any of us!"

Mister Packaday stacked his boxes in an apparent imitation of the Leaning Tower of Pisa, sighed enigmatically, and turned to face Bitty again. "I didn't think it was my responsibility. But it seemed to be wearing corrective underwear."

"Uncle Fleck!" theorized Bitty. "He *has* been missing!"

Young Doctor Salvage returned from the kitchen holding a large pair of hedge clippers.

"As near as I can tell from the autopsy," he said tersely, "your aunt failed to wash her hands after petting the cat. Infection was immediate."

"But she wasn't dead five minutes ago!" protested Bitty, her head beginning to spin like a washing machine full of mismatched whites and colors.

"By the way," the doctor continued. "I don't mean

to alarm you, but it seems as if your phone lines have been cut."

"A killer, or at any rate, fatal germs loose at Rancho Contento!" cried Anodyne. "This takes the cake for spooky!"

"Calm yourself," cautioned Bitty. "You know what perspiration stains do to your clothes!"

Surprisingly, it was the urbane Pilsener Packaday who suddenly panicked. "No phone! What if the pet store wants to reach me!"

"What are you talking about, Mister Packaday?" Bitty asked. "By the way, this is Blaine Salvage. Doctor, Pilsener Packaday."

The distracted author gathered his hatboxes and stumbled up the stairs to his room. "They're not going to get us! We're going away! Far away!"

"They? Us?" Bitty struggled to understand.

"I'll give him a sedative," Doctor Salvage said briskly. He opened his hedge clippers and followed Packaday up the stairs. "Smoking, no matter what they say, does not calm the nerves!"

Anodyne clutched Bitty in a frightened but non-suggestive manner. "Who's getting who, Bitty? And what's in those hatboxes?"

Before she could recap the story any further, the shadow of a figure filled the front doorway, which had been standing open since the doctor arrived. Anodyne jumped like a jackalope, but Bitty faced the intruder. It was Lazlo, the surly half-breed gardener. Nothing grew in the parched desert, which is one reason he was surly, but another might have been that years before, when he had first come to Rancho Contento, Lazlo had been sleepwalking, owing perhaps to his conflicted nationalities, and groggy Uncle Fleck had mistaken him for an intruder and shot him in the shoulder. Supposedly the incident was long forgotten, but at this moment Bitty wondered.

"Lazlo!" she breathed, as if to demonstrate she knew who he was.

"City man take my boxes," he said choppily. "I need boxes for debris. I must police area."

"Did Mister Packaday take your boxes, Lazlo?" Betty surmised. "Were they *hat* boxes, Lazlo?"

Doctor Salvage came back downstairs, his hair tousled and his lab coat wrinkled. "I'm afraid lung cancer has claimed your Mister Packaday," he announced impassively. "I think you'd all better come with me down to the airtight vault in the cellar."

"But what about the hatboxes?" Anodyne gurgled plaintively. "And— Oh!" A new horror swept over her like a forward stranger in a crowded elevator. "Bitty! The lights have gone out!"

Bitty quickly surveyed the room. "You're right! Luckily, it's two in the afternoon!"

"Just one second there!" barked Doctor Salvage with uncharacteristic emphasis. He had spied Lazlo sneaking up the stairs to Mister Packaday's room. "Where are you going?"

Lazlo turned, the lone feather in his headband drooping guiltily. "I need boxes—in case I have leaves to rake."

"There are no leaves in this wasteland," the doctor

shot back. He turned to Bitty. "Wait here, I'll go with him. I don't trust his mixed allegiances. Those bare feet suggest social discontent!"

He followed Lazlo out of sight up the not-so-brightly-lit-as-before staircase. The air tingled like an application of iodine.

"Bitty, this is Goosebump Central!" murmured Anodyne, nervously lighting a cigarette from the pack the late writer had left behind in his confusion.

"No, Anodyne, don't despair!" Bitty cried. "I'll call the sheriff's office from the pay phone by the waste site." She drew a coin from her pocket and stared at it in disbelief.

"Oh no! What's wrong?" Anodyne babbled, puffing smoke like a toaster nearing short-circuit.

"My dime has been *bent*," announced Bitty. "Making it useless in pay phone slots."

Upstairs, the sound of a scuffle made the antler chandeliers in the vestibule shake. Bitty reviewed the evidence.

"Anodyne, how could Aunt Addle have gotten herself so covered with cat hair in the old cavern?"

Doctor Salvage reappeared at the head of the stairs, as obsessed as a locomotive, and steamed down to the girls with the hatboxes in his arms. "I'm sorry to have to tell you this, but Lazlo seems to have succumbed to a rare case of fur balls in humans. His blood was more mixed than we knew."

"Hurry, let's see what's in those boxes!" shouted Anodyne, stubbing out her cigarette. The doctor glared at her disapprovingly.

"Wait a second, it occurs to me that Aunt Addle

had a threatening phone call last night," recalled Bitty suddenly.

Anodyne pulled the lid off one of the hatboxes and stared inside, at first with bewilderment, and then dismay. "Not more kittens! The ranch is overrun as it is, and there aren't mice enough for the ones we already have."

"Yes," Doctor Salvage said ominously. "Your Midnight has been a very, very careless animal, hasn't she?"

"Well, I—" Anodyne's blank face seemed perfectly to complement the benighted mewing that rose from the open hatbox.

"You don't even know who the father is, do you?" he continued, his voice as smooth and contained as a medicinal caplet.

Meanwhile, Bitty was absorbed in her real-life mental math. "Whoever it was must have been hysterical, because Aunt Addle got worked up herself. It was something about cycles of fornication, of profane and bestial horror, a rite of blood and rebirth."

"Bitty!" Anodyne called faintly, but powerful fingers on her throat prevented her from disrupting Bitty's concentration.

"Could Aunt Addle have taken Pilsener Packaday into her confidence? Where is Midnight, anyhow?"

"We must sterilize, sterilize all unclean substances!" young Doctor Salvage declared, releasing Anodyne's lifeless form to tumble to the floor with a drama unknown in her life. The sound of Anodyne's charm bracelet striking the parquet roused Bitty from her distraction. She beheld her late cousin, whom several of the now released kittens were vainly nuzzling, and turned to face Doctor Salvage. He stood stiffly in his torn lab coat, and his breathing sounded like a great skyscraper's heating ducts, soft but implicitly awesome in scope, and ineluctably mechanical.

"Well, Doctor," she said in as even a voice as she could muster. "If you insist, I will marry you."

THREE LOST POEMS

*(It is not generally known that Emily Dickinson worked
for a time as a copywriter at BBD&O, in Boston.)*

THE DOVE BAR

Some seek diviner Donuts
Who hear of Heaven's Sweets—
They pine for flying Crullers
Who dine on mundane Meats—

The Bird of Peace Transfigured—
Unconscious, on a Stick—
For once, a Fruit the haggard
And beggared Soul may pick—

The Arctic cream of Bossie—
That Aztec, Chocolate—
The White and Black made glossy—
And Justified—at that—

Antipodes united—
They must have used a Lab—
The polar Host has lighted—
The Word—a frozen Slab.

My heart could not accelerate—
It was weighed down by Fact.
Mere blood lacks petrol's octane
For speed's triumphal act.

The dead lie still while angels race;
The slow know death in life.
Velocity is Caesar—
It conquers like a knife.

I strove, in boots and bootless,
And neither made me fly.
Since Providence does not provide,
Then Commerce may comply.

This steed leaps from the foundry,
A stallion told in steel,
Exultant as the arrow
That soars above the Real.

Voracious clockwork panther,
Amnesiac in its climb,
It heedless fells the highway,
Remorseless—as Time.

| S O M I N E X |

———

Because Sleep tarried when I called,
And care gnawed at the walls,
I learned a faith in Chemistry,
The Djinn that answers calls.

Its powders spread like snowfall
Or all-obscuring sand,
Throughout the secret acres,
To still the fevered land.

The mob of thoughts disperses,
The wrenching pistons cease.
The greatest dream—is Dreamlessness—
The blizzard's whitening peace.

False robes of absolution,
Imposter's crown of rest—
The comfort of the blessed—here—
Conferred on the Unblessed.

DIARY OF A FAN

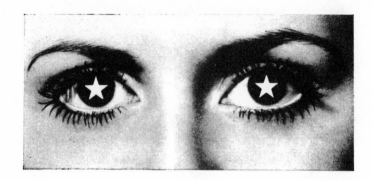

| S U N D A Y : |

I saw Sigourney Weaver on the street today. She was alone. I pity her.

Also—is this possible?—I think I saw Leslie Howard as a young man. It was near the Museum of Modern Art, so maybe he was there for one of their revivals.

———

Maurice at work wants to get serious. He sent me a Xerox copy of his face that he did in the mailroom. It was not flattering.

Lunch at the Chinese restaurant near the office. There were a lot of framed photos on the walls—struggling actors, I guess. They were all grinning like tigers, but their eyes were strictly deer caught in oncoming headlights. I asked the manager who they were, but all he could say was "Very famous." I think certain someones, or should I say certain nobodies, have been taking advantage of his recent-immigrant status. One man's photo I did recognize, but it was from seeing him at the newsstand where I get *Cahiers de la Célébrité*. He buys *Back Stage*, so how famous can he be?

After work I went to my Support for Lovers of Unattainably Remote People meeting. This week we met at Garbo Spooney's apartment. She's a second-generation fan (her mother dipped a handkerchief in Dillinger's blood), which I guess is what makes her so stuck-up. She has a framed picture of herself with the Invisible Man, but I suspect it's just an Invisible Man impersonator.

Right before the meeting began she asked if anyone was attending SLURP for the first time, when obviously it was the five of us, just like always.

"You don't have to be so formal, Garb," I told her.

I've been reading how successful people don't take guff.

"And you don't have to be so informal, *Sheel*," she said. Instead of Sheila. I guess she thought that was a comeback. "You might try wearing a dress or some makeup. Good grooming is the first step toward actual celebrity." I pity her. She still hasn't accepted that the Method and rock and roll changed all that forever.

Right after the meet-who-you-can-and-accept-not-meeting-Madonna pledge, one of the Cynthias (the one who works at the Bureau of Not Yet Missing Persons) started crying because she's finally faced the fact that Liz and Eddie will never reconcile. She's very slow at working these things through. Then the other Cynthia started crying about how hard it is to keep tabs on ex-Menudo members, especially since she doesn't speak Spanish. It's her own fault. If you're going to climb that mountain, you've got to do the work. No wonder real fans are a dying breed—people are getting too lazy for obsession.

Of course Garbo, in that condescending way of hers, tried to distract everyone by firing trivia questions at us. Not just the standard year-of-birth stuff, or even "Name the Seven Dwarfs," but "Name three or more rejected *suggestions* for the Seven Dwarfs' names." They're not strictly celebrities in the corporeal sense, so I resented it—especially with a Cynthia still crying—but Garbo just barreled ahead and rattled off a few, like Hungry and Brackish and Biggo Ego, and who could contradict her? Apparently she had an aunt who slept with a Disney animator. But, she always adds, all they did was sleep. There were studio rules.

I have to give that particular Cynthia credit—she did rally. She not only named the Seven Dwarfs (no big feat unless you're racked with sobs like she was) but got into a sort of ecstatic delirium and named the entire cast of *The Magnificent Seven*, including Horst Buchholz.

Then poor Gary with the two monocles started in again. He's hung up exclusively on the long-dead ones, like Cleopatra and Caruso. I tried to get him interested in Martha Stewart, but I think he *wants* to be hurt. At least it is *possible* I could meet Danny Sullivan. It is *possible* he would like me despite my problem ear, and change his ways. Gary is *never* going to meet Cleopatra, unless you believe in a Heaven where Cleopatra has lost all sense of standards. I told him to face the real world. He started crying then, too. All in all, a good meeting.

Message on my machine from Maurice: Do I want to go to a party with famous scientists on Saturday? Do I like them? Someone in Toxics invited him. I want to be all I can be, but I don't want to mislead Maurice.

| T U E S D A Y : |

———

Saw Sigourney Weaver on the street again, on my way to work. She was with a couple of people who were talking intensely. They must want something from her. I feel sorry for her.

After our fire drill turned out to be real, I walked home via Broadway, past the OTB, and I think I saw Dr. Robert Jarvik, the artificial-heart man who's married to the real brain, but I'm not sure. My medical knowledge is spotty. It may have been that dentist who poses in the underwear ad. I have much to learn.

| W E D N E S D A Y : |

———

Had to go to the mailroom for Liquid Paper. Maurice still wants to get serious, but I told him I'd never heard of him, except from him, though once I saw his name posted on the United Way Delinquency Donor sheet. He said that at least *he'd* heard of *me*, and we could build on that. I told him it would be like a tree being famous in the woods when no one's around. He just stood there, kind of bathed in flashes of green light from the Xerox machine. He said I was dazzled by the sunlight on a swimming pool I'd never own, and then he pounded his fist on the postage meter ($3.40 wasted) and called me a groupie. How quickly love turns to hate! Look at the young royals and whoever.

On the way home I thought I saw Matt Dillon's stand-in, but it turned out to be Johnny Depp's alternate stunt double. He said he believes he's the reincarnation of James Dean's stunt double, but people mistake him for the movie version of Dondi, the later years. I didn't give him my number. He seems to have a few things to work out.

The corner stationery store doesn't carry autograph

books anymore. The clerk said they went out with culottes. I told him culottes were back, but I was shaken.

Dreamed I went to Hell but no one was there, not even the Devil. Is that the point?

| T H U R S D A Y : |

———

I saw Sigourney Weaver on the street *again*. Maybe she isn't so famous after all.

| F R I D A Y : |

———

Big date last night that went bust. I met a British-sounding guy in Tower Records's Accounts Overdue line who turned out to be a distant cousin of Sting's. He calls himself Chafe. Anyway, he suggested dinner later on, and in my nervousness all I could think of was the Chinese place near work. He was late— something about a conference call to rehearse his band—so I'd gone ahead and ordered. We chatted for a while about England (he'd like to go there someday), but he started getting impatient for the food, so he threw a tantrum, which isn't attractive if there are no paparazzi around. He even tried storm- ing out, but there was a party of six coming in and he had to wait for them to get by.

I sat there having a career crisis for a second. I'm sick of dating entry-level celebs and will-have-had- beens. Maybe I should move to a small town and follow the career of the local livestock. Anyway, Chafe came slinking back in to get his knapsack, and he must have sensed my disenchantment, because suddenly I was attractive to him again. He invited me to go to Fata Morgana with him—this was the night the club was going from hip to unhip, so we could watch the dance floor empty. I said no, and he got desperate and said he was also Meat Loaf's estranged brother, Casserole. I could feel the eyes of the unknowns burning into me from the framed glossies, and I excused myself to go to the bathroom. I didn't tell him it was the bathroom back at my house.

Had a rough night. I woke up reciting Mr. Blackwell's "Best Dressed" List. That was odd, because I dreamed I was naked and had no place to put my autograph book.

| SATURDAY: |

———

I shouldn't have, but I let Maurice take me to this reception in the Van Leeuwenhoek Room at the Sheraton, the NSF's annual ceremony to honor the Element of the Year—"that building block of matter that has most touched the hearts of the scientific community in the past twelve months." I guess I'm as corrupt as anyone, because I ditched Maurice right after the shrimp cocktail arranged like the space embryo in *2001*. I said I had to phone my Gabor Update Service. I soon regretted it, because basically the scene was a bunch of bald guys throwing objects in the hotel pool and predicting the ripple effects.

The award itself seems to be totally unrelated to merit. Hydrogen was up for it—you'd think it was a shoo-in, being in air and water and all—but somebody said it was perceived as too lightweight. Boron was nominated, but it has no publicity machine at all, and a lot of people think it's a compound. Maurice's friend from Toxics said Krypton was hot, with all this Superman mania, but I bet him my sherbet in the shape of a Necker cube that Carbon would get it, since that basis-of-all-life thing gives it some human interest. But you know what won? Gold. It made me sick.

I was too ashamed to go sit with Maurice again, but he found me by the cold-fusion table and said he'd drive me home. We didn't talk the whole way. The stars were out, but I'm tired of them. Balls of gases—that's all they are.

SUNDAY:

I was restless, and got up early to take a walk. I didn't see Sigourney Weaver all day, and I even hung out by her bank machine. She must be trying to make a comeback. Poor Sigourney. I'm through with her.

Maurice left a message on my machine that I got at bedtime. A wandering newspaper photographer had asked him if he thought ours was a world of skewed values. I forget if he said it was or not, but his picture will be in Tuesday's paper. It occurs to me that Maurice has beautiful eyes. Patient and tender. Kind of like Benji's.

ILLUSTRATION BREAK

"Do you not be happy with me as the translator of the books of you?"

"Fine, Mr. and Mrs. . . . ahem . . . Dog. The bellboy will show you to your room."

EXTINCTION of the DINOSAURS FULLY EXPLAINED

"... Yeah, he done me wrong, but I got over it.... I had it bad, but I'm better now...."

DRAGNET HAIKU

Eleven fifty seven p.m.--
the white chrysanthemum.

The GUEST TOWELS of TURIN

" . . . Well now, let's see here. I'd say you folks were just about a few feet away, right here at the county fair. Am I close?"

GUESS WHO'S PSYCHIC

DEAR MR. CABAL—

I don't believe in psychics or psychiatry, and sometimes I even doubt physics, but just in case, I am sending you a contribution. Will it change my luck even if I'm not sure it will? I've had peck after peck of nothing but bad apples. I could try not to doubt you.

Panhandle Pegleg

Many, or anyway, you, are prey to doubt. I sense your aura is an uninvited guest in the House of Atlantis, and the rule there is He Who Doubts Must Not Be Spoken To. Yet, I am speaking to you, or anyway, addressing you in my column. That must reveal something to you.

DEAR MR. CABAL—

When I had my nose job, I wrote to you wondering if I would survive. I didn't hear from you but I figured you sent out your helpful vibrations without fanfare. After all, I'd had several small problems you cleared up without my even having to write to you. Guess what, I survived! And now I have a beautiful little baby nose which is the light of my life—and my husband's. How can I ever thank you?

Peachy in Alberta

Your accompanying donation is all the thanks I needed or expected.

DEAR MR. CABAL—

My friend John (not his real name) and I (I am also named John, though not really, because I've changed our matching names to still match) seem to be on a close psychic wavelength, and it scares me. For example, last summer, during the heat wave, I phoned him and it turned out we were both sipping cold water. His was bottled, but it was the same beverage. Last week I saw him at the muffler replacement center. We were both having our mufflers replaced. When the bills came, they were identical. Then on Friday we ran into each other and ran out of chat, and there was a silence, and then we both said, "Well, have a nice weekend!" At the same time, nearly. The burden of a bond like this is frightening. What can I do to keep from merging with him into a four-armed blob? And what if it doesn't merge exactly right and we only have one-and-a-half heads or something? That would make it even harder to find work.

One Guy, for Now

It won't happen. I can sense your two energies completing a sort of goodwill "jamboree" they've been having together, and now they're going in skew directions. You're safe. For extra security, start calling yourself Jack, or whatever is the equivalent nickname for your real name, which I know perfectly well.

DEAR MR. CABAL—
I have written to you many times, and my problems have never seemed interesting enough to answer in your column, so this time I am including a stamped, self-addressed envelope along with my donation, so you can answer me without boring your readers. The people where I work must hate me, but they cover it with smiles and nice gifts. Here's a photo of us all at the last Christmas party. I'm the one everyone's kissing. What can you pick up about their real hatred? Can they be stopped?

Secretly Stung in the
International Bank of The
Hague

Thank you for your contribution. They like you now.

DEAR MR. CABAL—

If you're so psychic, I don't even have to tell you
my problem, do I?

Betcha I Gotcha

No, you don't.

DEAR MR. CABAL—

I was in Thailand recently, looking for my father,
a mercenary whom I've never met. I was stranded
in a small airport during a monsoon and was struck
by a piece of flying luggage. While I was unconscious, a great Siamese cat came to me and said I
would recover. I realized it was a dream so I didn't
bother to ask it any serious questions like where
my father was or life's whole point. Sure enough,
though, I regained consciousness. It turned out I'd
been struck by a flying cat carrier. There hadn't
been a cat in it, but if there had, it probably
wouldn't have had the altitude or velocity to strike
me. Now I wonder if I should try to get hit by
another piece of luggage and ask the right questions this time. Would it have to be the same cat
carrier? Is it considered cheating to try to set up
these things? Would I be taunted for my presumption once I'd lost consciousness? What if, since I'd
be insensible, I forgot to ask the right questions?
I'd hate to go to the trouble, then. Also, I might
get killed if something else in the wind hits me.

New Cat Fancier

I think you've answered your own question.

DEAR MR. CABAL—
I get this powerful feeling that there is a parallel universe in which I'm a super-warlock ruler, and people there like me. I do magic from my throne and they invite me to sit with them after. I can't seem to get to this parallel universe, however, and I worry about my kingdom there going unsupervised. My people must miss me.

The King of Somewhere

I projected my inner beam and found your kingdom in a very charming little parallel universe, and all is well there. It's one of those rare worlds in which everything runs fine without rulers or even magic. Your subjects send their best, but they don't need you. Don't worry about it. Get it off your mind. Live in the world you're in.

THE STATE OF THE HATE

I was recently a guest at a dinner party hosted by a friend, Janet X (her real name, strangely enough; she blames a careless male registrar at Ellis Island). Owing to a string of coincidences, the husbands and boyfriends invited had stayed home to watch the Super Bowl, and I was the only man in a group that otherwise included four women. Despite the thick shag of my masculine oblivion, though maybe I'm flattering myself there, I still sensed tension, like in those deco thrillers where one of the period house-guests must be the murderer. I guessed it to be residual rankling from the afternoon seminar on the Duties of Venereal Disobedience all of them had attended earlier at our local Pottery Barn. Furthermore, the keynote speaker at the seminar also happened to be the guest of honor at Janet's dinner, and all cocktail glasses tipped toward her in anticipation.

She was the notorious but here nameless (in fact, everywhere nameless; she, too, blamed the man at Ellis Island) author of a best-selling trilogy on erotic insurgence, *Date Hate*; its follow-up, *Mate Hate*; and her latest, *Ex Hex*, loud volumes that had sent revolutionary ripples across many a steno pool. She was the last word in blonded misanthropy, and had just made headlines by decking her own grandfather at a press conference for calling her Honey ("That's something fat male bears eat!"). In the wake of such a fomentress, and in any case flash-stapled to her celebrity, I was hotly self-conscious, like a living tableau of Testosterone Captive Before Athena.

At first I tried to amuse the company with the harmless old clip-on bowtie routine, playing multiple stock roles as I switched voices and the bowtie from hairbow position to mustache to collar: "I *can't* pay the rent!" "You *must* pay the rent!" "*I'll* pay the rent!" It didn't go over as well as it always had at camp, and Janet even pointed out that Hairbow might have paid the rent for Collar, that I had overlooked that possibility. I did it again that way, but it was wearing thin, and besides, I'm thirty-three years old.

Then I tried to talk to the famous yet nameless author, though I had to catch her eye to get her attention because of her namelessness. In a conciliatory spirit, I asked her if her grandmother didn't ever call her Honey.

"My grandmother is dead," she answered with piercing flatness, if physics allows such a medley.

"Typical," one of the other women responded.

I might have pointed out that women live longer than men, but it didn't seem an opportune moment. I tried a friendly gambit instead. "Well, you do get first crack at the lifeboats!" I smiled, but no one matched me, and I was left with paradoxically masculine egg on my face.

At last the meal ended, and we decompressed over coffee and rich slices of LaBrea fudge decadence cake. I had just finished innocently observing that I could eat all I wanted of anything and never gain weight, when I noticed the assembly looking at me with no longer concealed hostility, as if I were the flippant meteorologist who once named hurricanes after women. Hoping to defuse any ticking ill will, I raised my vocal register slightly, involuntarily but I hoped as a gesture of solidarity, and asked for another piece of the cake.

"You sure outdid yourself baking this!" I offered as I helped myself, hoping to show men don't have to be waited on.

"She didn't bake it, she bought it," the woman next to me commented tersely, seeming to foam at the edges like an ovum under the microscope. She had been divorced several months before, and had reverted to her mother's maiden name, effectively divorcing her father into the bargain. I had inadvertently got on her wrong side by pointing out that she still bore a man's last name, and would have to reach back through countless generations to unyoke herself, and when she finally got to Eve, there would be no last name to adopt.

"Typical," she had said.

I nervously shoveled a forkful of LaBrea cake into my mouth, and impetuously chose the same moment to grin ingratiatingly. Another of the women stared at me with what my father used to call the Furry Eyeball. "*Men,*" she said at last. "*They're both alike.*"

Her statement disconcerted me, but then I remembered that she was a widow's only child who had been schooled in a girls' convent, and only recently had broken up with her first serious boyfriend, a taciturn hulk who refused to explore his feelings with her, no matter how simple the questionnaires she submitted to him, and who could never, it seemed, be reached at work (he is a well-known race car driver).

I shifted uneasily and realized my praise for the dessert might have seemed condescending, especially since Janet hadn't baked it herself. I tried to make up to her without admitting I'd offended. "I have to admit—" I groped. "Not many men would know where to buy a delicious cake like that!"

My concession wafted miserably to the floor, and the women looked at each other and rolled their eyes. I sensed the yin was about to hit the yang.

"Don't you ever get tired of causing pain?" the writer asked me pointedly, and added, "Quick, yes or no?"

I knew neither answer would get me off the hook gracefully, and although it may have been a constriction in my throat, I was sure I heard a tumbril creak outside the apartment door. Suddenly, and conveniently, I remembered a boulder-rolling invitational sponsored by a men's deodorant that was to take me north to Halifax immediately, by railway handcar and under cover of darkness. In my haste, I left behind my clip-on bowtie, blazon of false forgetful he-hood. I haven't returned to New York since. I suppose, in its way, it was a typical male response.

KIDS' MOST-ASKED QUESTIONS ABOUT ELECTRICITY

Answers to Questions Kids Might Ask GE Mascot Reddy Kilowatt During His Tour of American Elementary Schools

Q: Is that light-bulb head supposed to be cute?
A: *You'll have to ask my designers, but I believe it's supposed to be indirectly educational.*

Q: What, as if we never saw a light bulb before?
A: *Not everyone has had your advantages.*

Q: Why are your arms all crooked?
A: *They're bolts of energy.*

Q: Do you have a penis?
A: No.

Q: So, are you from outer space or what?
A: No, I'm just a drawing.

Q: Can I get a suit like yours?
A: You wouldn't be skinny or zigzag enough to wear it.

Q: I know fire isn't exactly electric, but what about flame throwers? Or bazookas? How about bombs? Are they electric? Or are you just to help Mom's blender make yogurt shakes for babies?
A: All the things you mention have electric components.

Q: What about those giant robots that Godzilla fights? Are they alive?
A: As a form of brute nature, I'm unqualified to comment on the dramatic arts.

Q: Is it satisfying to flow through the body of a condemned killer?
A: No, I'm emotionless. As lightning, I strike innocent forest rangers and prairie housewives, too.

Q: What happens if you touch water? Do you die?
A: Electricity does not conceive of its own cessation.

Q: What about "sexual electricity"? Is it really electricity?
A: I'm answering children's questions only, sir.

Q: They always show atomic energy with big muscles. You must be jealous, huh?
A: *I don't get a chance to look at other drawings.*

Q: Why is it we get wax in our ears and snot in our nose? Why not snot in the ears and wax in the nose? Why not the same thing in both places?
A: *That's a biological matter, to which I'm indifferent. I only* seem *to live.*

Q: So if I waste electricity, like, by leaving the lights on all night, do you go lie down somewhere and weep?
A: *No. You're thinking of Christ.*

Q: I don't think you're neat. I think you're queer.
A: *That's not a question.*

Q: Let me get this straight. Does it mean your nose and your stomach and your gloves and all of you are made of nothing but energy?
A: *Believe it or not, kid, so are you.*

BARTLETT'S FAMILIAR
QUOTATIONS: THE PLAY

*(The scene: A dingy, threadbare apartment not unlike the
Kramdens', in a quietly desperate neighborhood in a city not
unlike Brooklyn. It is a dreary dawn, about six a.m. On a
couch in one corner of this room, which serves as both kitchen
and living room, lies a figure in a dressing gown with a
newspaper over his face. He is barely noticeable and may go
unnoticed until he first speaks. After a few moments,* **HATTIE**
*enters, looking haggard and sleepless. She has been up all
night, and although she may be pretty at her best, the dark
weight of thirty-plus years of trouble besets her. She glances
at the wall clock miserably, and grimaces at the sound of
reckless garbagemen in the street below. She coughs, a serious
hacking cough, and limps to a rusted dryer in a far corner.
She opens its porthole door and pulls out a wet shirt from
among a tangle of still-damp laundry. She wrings it out and
water trickles to the floor. This is the last straw. She weeps.)*

(From the next room a toilet is heard flushing. **HATTIE** *pauses. Several seconds pass, and* **PLATO** *enters. Yes, he wears the robes of classical antiquity, but here he is a pretentious freeloader, a smug dignitary assured that his hosts are honored to have him. He stretches and peers out the window, over the tenement rooftops, at the rising light.)*

PLATO: The morn! . . . Look you . . . furthers a man on his road, and furthers him too in his work!

*(****HATTIE*** *stares at him in bewilderment. After a few moments, she cries afresh.)*

By suffering comes wisdom!

(She does not respond, but turns away from him. The clock strikes six.)

It is for the doer to suffer!

*(****HATTIE*** *rolls her eyes at this platitude, stands, and awkwardly tries to hang the wet shirt up to dry from a curtain rod.* **PLATO** *gives her one more axiom as she struggles.)*

He who is of a calm and happy nature will hardly feel the pressure of age, but to him who is of an opposite disposition, youth and age are equally a burden!

*(****HATTIE*** *eyes him fiercely, a dagger of resentment. He shrugs and turns his attention to the stove, where he fusses with assorted utensils in preparation for breakfast. He lifts a frying pan and thoughtfully addresses it.)*

Ah, beloved Pan!

*(He sets it down and goes to the refrigerator for eggs and bacon. **HATTIE** angrily intervenes and closes the refrigerator door, placing herself between him and the groceries. He sighs.)*

Poverty is the parent of meanness and discontent.

*(From offstage comes the wail of an infant. **HATTIE** groans and exits limping to her baby. **PLATO** seizes this opportunity to get grub from the icebox.)*

Of all the animals, the boy is the most unmanageable!

(He opens an egg carton and sees there is only one left. He shrugs.)

It is better to have a little than nothing.

(He cracks the egg in the pan, turns on the flame beneath it, and takes several slices of bread from an open package. The child's cry is heard again from offstage.)

Man alone . . . cast naked upon the naked earth, does she abandon to cries and lamentations!

*(He stuffs a slice of bread in his mouth and puts two others in the toaster. **HATTIE** reenters with a swaddled bundle we presume to be her child. She sees **PLATO** helping himself and glares. He grins as if charmingly and swallows the mouthful of bread.)*

Ahh! A great step toward independence is a good-natured stomach!

*(She grabs the bag of bread he is holding and turns off the flame under the frying pan. She carries the baby to a nearby basket and lays it there to sleep. As she does, **PLATO** defends himself.)*

Socrates says, "Bad men live that they may eat and drink, whereas good men eat and drink that they may live."

*(**HATTIE** stares the old windbag down in withering Alice Kramden fashion.)*

HATTIE: Shut up!

*(Awkward moment. **PLATO** gathers himself and makes a pettish observation.)*

PLATO: What is the prime of life? May it not be defined in a woman's life at about . . . twenty years?

*(She could brain him for this, and picks up a rolling pin, but a coughing fit seizes her, and then, lumbering male noise is heard at the door. A key rattles in the lock, and the door opens, revealing **GEORGE**, **HATTIE**'s utterly soused lout of a husband. Lipstick kisses decorate his flushed face, and his clothes are wrinkled. He leaves the door open, and staggers in, giggling. **HATTIE** collars him angrily.)*

PLATO *(warily)*: An overtaxed patience gives way to fury!

*(This is a personal problem, so **PLATO** turns away, to the kitchen counter. **HATTIE** shakes **GEORGE** furiously, but he just giggles helplessly.)*

A fit of laughter which has been indulged to excess almost always produces a violent reaction.

*(**PLATO**'s toast pops up. He removes, butters and eats it, all as the couple wrangle close at hand. They jostle him inadvertently, so he feels compelled to advise them again.)*

Submit to the present evil, lest a greater one befall you!

(At this bromide, the supine character on the couch stirs, removes his newspaper covering, and sits up. It is LA ROCHEFOUCAULD, the seventeenth-century author of maxims, plummy and foppish, self-delighted, deliberate and sly, in a full peruke. He addresses PLATO as a lesser competitor.)

LA ROCHEFOUCAULD: Nothing is given so profusely . . . as advice!

(He puckers his lips, as if to say "Touché!" HATTIE and GEORGE tumble over the couch as they fight. GEORGE is no longer laughing, but gasping for breath as HATTIE tries to strangle him. LA ROCHE-FOUCAULD clucks his tongue.)

Philosophy triumphs easily over past evils and future evils, but present evils triumph over it!

(HATTIE grabs a large kitchen knife and stalks GEORGE, who tries a new tack by weeping crocodile tears.)

GEORGE: Honey, I'm sorry! I'm sorry!

LA ROCHEFOUCAULD: Hmph! Hypocrisy is the homage that vice pays to virtue.

(Amazingly, HATTIE is touched by GEORGE's contrition. Panting and heaving, they embrace. Suddenly, however, she finds a long blond hair on his shoulder.)

PLATO: Even a single hair casts its shadow! *(Pause. He cites his source.)* Publilius Syrus.

(The fight resumes. HATTIE breaks a bottle over GEORGE's head. He falls to his knees, but she leaps to

his throat and begins to strangle him. He collapses, and she pauses.)

LA ROCHEFOUCAULD: Jealousy feeds upon suspicion, and it turns into fury—or it ends as soon as it passes from suspicion to certainty.

*(**HATTIE** straddles her fallen husband and ponders momentarily. Will her passion pass? Instead of recovering, though, she suddenly goes at him with renewed vehemence, violently pounding his head against the floor. Then, just as suddenly, she stops, seized with the realization of what she is doing. **GEORGE** lies ominously still. Fearfully, she puts her ear to his chest to listen for his heart.)*

HATTIE: Oh my God!!

*(**LA ROCHEFOUCAULD** huddles with **PLATO** for safety.)*

LA ROCHEFOUCAULD: Our repentance is not so much regret for the ill we have done as fear for the ill that may happen to us in consequence.

HATTIE: George! . . . *(**GEORGE** briefly regains consciousness. After a tense pause, he speaks, slowly and with difficulty, in bursts.)*

GEORGE: Who . . . are . . . those . . . guys? . . . *(He dies.)*

HATTIE: I thought they were friends of yours! *(She collapses weeping on his body.)*

PLATO *(to console her)*: The soul of man is immortal and imperishable.

*(This nugget of nobility clinches the title as far as he's concerned, and he simpers defiantly at **LA ROCHEFOU-***

CAULD *over* **HATTIE**'s *head.* **LA ROCHEFOUCAULD**
stares at his rival unimpressed.)

LA ROCHEFOUCAULD: We all have strength enough
to endure the misfortunes of others.

*(***PLATO*** decides to overlook this feeble cut.)*

PLATO: You are young, my son, and therefore, refrain
a while from setting yourself up as a judge of the
highest matters.

(This petty, mock-patient debate is broken up by **HAT-
TIE**'s *sudden, feverish, even hypnotic recovery. She bolts
upright with feral urgency. For a moment she turns
away from* **GEORGE**'s *corpse to figure out some log-
istics.)*

LA ROCHEFOUCAULD: Neither the sun nor death can
be looked at constantly.

*(***HATTIE*** drags* **GEORGE**'s *body into the other room.
As she disappears,* **WILLA CATHER** *pokes her head in
through the open door. She wears a simple country dress
and the tastefully worn expression of a classic pioneer
novelist, but here she functions as a curious next-door
neighbor, concerned about the commotion. She has
flour-whitened hands, from the bread dough she has
been kneading in her kitchen.)*

*(***HATTIE*** returns, possessed and wild-eyed.* **WILLA**,
who is an earnest drag, looks to **HATTIE** *for an explanation. Pause.)*

HATTIE *(finally)*: I killed him!! But I didn't mean to!!

*(She falls to her knees in mad, brief, presuicidal prayer.
She is beyond chatting with boarders and neighbors now.*

*WILLA recovers from her surprise, and regards **HAT-TIE** with strong, patronizing grace, like an old-fashioned teacher.)*

WILLA: Sometimes, a neighbor we have disliked . . . lets fall a single commonplace remark that shows us another side . . . Another person, really . . . Uncertain, and puzzled, and in the dark like ourselves.

*(**HATTIE** babbles incomprehensible prayers.)*

The Miracles of the Church seem to me to rest upon our perceptions being made finer, so that for a moment our eyes can see and our ears can hear what is there about us always.

(She nods to her sage cohorts, a tad piously.)

LA ROCHEFOUCAULD *(tartly)*: Old people like to give good advice. It is solace for not being able to provide bad examples.

*(**WILLA** is basically impervious to this remark, and anyway, **HATTIE** stands up suddenly and stumbles to the window. She has ceased even noticing her guests. She climbs onto the ledge desperately, and is seized with another coughing fit, one last reminder of earthly travail.)*

HATTIE: I'm sorry!!

(From the street below, we hear excited voices, a crowd assembling. Spectators call up to her anxiously.)

VOICE OF GOETHE: Miss, don't! Calmly wait the morrow's hidden season!

VOICE OF WORDSWORTH: Look for the stars! The rainbow comes and goes, and lovely is the Rose!

VOICE OF ROBERT LEY: Strength Through Joy!

VOICE OF ERNEST HEMINGWAY: The world is a fine place and worth fighting for!

AN ANONYMOUS VOICE: Jump!

VOICE OF CARL SANDBURG: I am the people! The mob! The crowd! The mass! Do you know that all the great work of the world is done through me?

AN ANONYMOUS VOICE: Jump!

*(**HATTIE**, miserable and confused, turns in to seek advice from the trio inside. She looks to them beseechingly.)*

PLATO *(to his companions)*: Human beings live in a cave. They see only their shadows, or the shadows of one another, which the fire throws on the walls of the cave.

*(**WILLA** and **LA ROCHEFOUCAULD** murmur and nod. Their complacence dismays **HATTIE**, and she begins to bawl like Lucille Ball. She turns back outward. The three visitors look at each other as if they've done all they can, and shrug.)*

VOICE OF FRANKLIN ROOSEVELT: We have nothing to fear but fear itself!

*(But it's too late. **HATTIE** jumps. Screams and uproar from the street below cover the sound of her tragic landing.)*

WILLA: There are only two or three human stories, and they go on repeating themselves as fiercely as if they had never happened before.

*(A low siren is heard approaching in the distance. It makes **PLATO** uneasy. He goes to the radio and turns it on.)*

LA ROCHEFOUCAULD: We may give advice, but we do not inspire conduct.

(He opens the abandoned bread package, takes out a slice, butters and eats it. The radio produces incongruous dance music, so **PLATO** *tunes it to another station. After a moment of static, he finds an interview show.)*

VOICE OF FRANKLIN PIERCE ADAMS:

Go, little booke!

and let who will be clever!

Roll on! From yonder ivy-mantled tower

the moon and I could keep this up forever!

A VOICE FROM THE STREET:

Who saw her die?

I, said the Fly!

With my little eye!

I saw her die!

(The siren stops. **LA ROCHEFOUCAULD** *munches on his bread.* **CHRIST** *appears in the window and grins in at the three assembled thinkers.* **PLATO** *reflexively turns off the radio.* **CHRIST** *speaks enthusiastically—almost singing, like Baby June Hovick—but rather jarringly, like a bad actor delivering the wrong line with great cheerful conviction.)*

CHRIST:

I am His Majesty's dog at Kew!

Pray tell me, sir, whose dog are YOU???

*(***CHRIST*** grins, and the baby awakes and cries. Blackout.)*

THE GIRL WHO DATED
THE MOON

The Hopi Indians, or at least some people who live out that way, tell the story of a willful girl who took it into her head to date the moon. Despite the protests of her parents, she invited the celestial body to her family home. Needless to say, what she expected to be an overwhelming experience proved to be a disappointment.

First of all, the moon turned out to have no light of its own, a disillusioning fact that was all too evident when it finally did arrive, a mere dark rock with no glow at all, and hours late because in dislodging itself from its orbit it had altered the very basis of time-keeping and confused even itself. Secondly, it was nothing in size like its seeming equal, the sun, which is a million times larger than the earth. Frankly, the moon was scarcely the diameter of the United States. And, of course, at close quarters its mysterious and provocative imperfections were deep jagged canyons and ridges.

After a few fitful attempts at conversation, the girl fell silent. Her infatuation had been instantly shattered, and indeed, she hated the moon. However, it was too late. The moon had fallen for her, hard, and her indifference after inviting it such a great distance teased and obsessed it. It is a mere rock, remember. The moon began to pursue the girl around the grounds, but she turned into a Coleman lantern to escape his notice. (It should be mentioned that she possessed the power to turn herself into anything at will, a talent she had so overly indulged as to lead to her disorientation. That probably explains how she became so addled as to ask the moon out in the first place.)

The moon eventually noticed that there was a Coleman lantern it hadn't noticed before, so the girl quickly transformed herself into a hare, a broomstick, the shingles on the gardening shed, and even a set of second-mortgage papers, but the moon knew enough, if not to see through each successive disguise, to realize it was getting the runaround. Its love turned suddenly to hate; these things happen even in astronomical circles, and it swore it would kill her when she stopped transforming. At this point her parents asked it to leave, and as it ascended into the sky, it vowed it would never return, and it never has.

At hearing his vow, the girl turned back into herself and ran out onto the lawn to taunt the moon as it receded, an unnecessarily cruel fillip, but she was willful and that is what happened.

After his stinging rejection, from that day to this, the moon has had phases, and you certainly must be able to sympathize with that.

THE ART OF FICTITIOUSNESS

A N I N T E R V I E W W I T H

S A M U E L B E C K E T T

Samuel Beckett, born in Dublin in 1906 and a resident of Paris since 1937, is the author of the trilogy of novels Molloy, Malone Meurt, *and* L'Innomable, *and the plays* En Attendant Godot, Fin de Partie (Endgame), Happy Days *(not the television series), and numerous others. The one you've read,* Waiting for Godot, *was staged in America with Bert Lahr, who played the Cowardly Lion in* The Wizard of Oz.

It must be said that Beckett looks all of his eighty years, and during our interview progressed from a kind of charged, essential silence into a state of sullen resentfulness, and finally, of despair. He wore a worn dressing gown throughout our conversation at his Paris flat, although on several occasions he did attempt to get dressed. There were no refreshments served, not even coffee.

Beckett: *Qui est là?*
Interviewer: Candygram!
Beckett: *Qu'est-ce que c'est?*
Interviewer: You don't have to speak in French, Mr. Beckett. I'm an American.
Beckett: I didn't order any candy.
Interviewer: And you aren't getting any. Excuse me, it was drafty out in the corridor. Shall we sit down?
Beckett: I don't understand.
Interviewer: SHALL I SPEAK MORE LOUDLY?
Beckett: I don't understand what you're doing here.
Interviewer: I'd say I'm a fan of your writing, but given its blasted-beyond-frippery starkness, that would be fatuous. I'd say I was a devotee except that sounds like I'd commit murder if you asked me to. Speaking of stark, this isn't the most upholstered chair I ever sat in.
Beckett: I'm very tired, and I'm not feeling well.
Interviewer: May I observe something? You sound like one of your characters.
Beckett: I will not be interviewed against my will.
Interviewer: You're crusty, Mr. Beckett, you're a regular character. I'm Irish, too, you know. Well, Irish American. Anyway, my dad's dad was Irish. My

mother's family came from Yugoslavia. With my red hair everyone thinks I'm Irish, though, even though in the summer it's more blond. Once this bum on the street who was drunk called me a Nazi rat. In a way it's not a compliment but I figured he thought I was blond.

Beckett: This cannot continue.

Interviewer: See, there you go again! It sounds like something out of that play where they're buried up to their necks in—wait a second, I guess it's just one woman. There's one with urns where they're stuck in urns and they do the whole play twice and you mention Lipton tea, I figure you get a big kickback from Lipton every time they do that one, huh? I'm a playwright, too, I get obscure prizes too, and like you, I'm too far out for Broadway or movie deals. I had one play that was optioned for the movies but you can imagine how that turned out. You know all about mortal misery, huh?

Beckett: I'm discovering more all the time.

Interviewer: See, you're worried that I'm some crazy student who has to write a thesis on you and wants to get some tidbit out of you he can milk into a stack of articles, and I don't. You probably secretly laugh at everyone who tries to analyze your stuff for meaning, and don't worry, I'm not going to do that. I don't even think Godot is God; I think he's anything that will provide an answer. Quick, yes or no?

Beckett: I can't oblige you, I have to see my doctor this morning.

Interviewer: Oh, Sam, stop fishing, you look fine! May I call you Sam? I could call you Mister Beckett. Or Samuel. You know the old joke about the kid who says his name is Sam and the teacher says, What's the rest of it? and he says, Mule. Sam-mule, get it? An American kind of joke, I guess.

Beckett: I have to see my doctor, you can't stay.

Interviewer: You have to get over this shyness, Mister Beckett, if as an impartial observer I can just offer my un-phony opinion. But maybe you like to surround yourself with flatterers, I don't know.

Beckett: Don't you understand? I'm not feeling well.

Interviewer: Okay, I'll play along. You look fine, Mister Beckett, just fine! You know that joke about there being three stages of life, Youth, Middle Age, and Gee You Look Good?

Beckett: I'll call the concierge.

Interviewer: I can always talk to him later, but I thought I'd talk to you first and then get what everyone really thinks of you behind your back after that. Though some coffee would be nice. Does the concierge serve coffee? We don't have servants in America, or I don't, at least, not that I begrudge you yours. At your age I think you're entitled to some kind of help. What are you, like eighty-something?

Beckett: Please stop.

Interviewer: I keep forgetting about that show business ego of yours. Believe me, I'm on your side. You're a survivor, and that rates any kind of didoes you want to pull, in my book. Oh, oops, sorry, this vase, you shouldn't have put—

Beckett: It's nothing, forget it, please go.

Interviewer: Ow, I cut myself on one of the pieces!

Beckett: I'll call the housekeeper.

Interviewer: No, it isn't really cut. I thought it was, but . . . it's not.

Beckett: Are you all right?

Interviewer: Now, let's not get this turned around! I'm asking the questions. It's my interview of you, after all. What does it matter if I'm all right? Let's leave me out of this! You're the man of the hour here. I've always wanted to interview you, I pitched you at the last magazine I worked for, *Tiger Beat*; I don't know if you're familiar with it?

Beckett: No.

Interviewer: They had never even heard of you, can you tie that? My editor-in-chief says to me, "You mean like a Whatever Happened To on that cute kid?" And I said to him, "Cute kid? Do you know what Samuel Beckett *looks* like?" Turns out he was thinking of *Scotty* Beckett! Do you know who that is?

Beckett: No.

Interviewer: Scotty Beckett was a child actor of the thirties and forties. He was in "Our Gang" for a while and he played the young Jolson in *The Jolson Story*. Everybody is always saying Larry Parks, Larry Parks whenever they talk about *The Jolson Story*, and they forget that Scotty Beckett is in it, too, at the beginning. And there's *Thomas* à Becket, too. They did a play about him. That must confuse some people.

Beckett: I beg of you, it's so early—

Interviewer: Yes, what's this myth about writers working in the morning? I came early to make sure I caught you, but it is a little disillusioning to find you in your nightgown, though if you really are as old as you say you must need a lot of rest. Don't think I'm criticizing, believe me, nobody likes your writing more than I do. We even did *Waiting for Godot* in my high school. Except our drama teacher said, No way, that we'd do *You Can't Take It With You* again, and I had had just about enough, so we formed this little splinter group to do wild stuff our drama teacher wouldn't like. The problem was nobody else understood it, even the actors I got to do it, plus since we were unofficial we couldn't advertise or have a budget, so it kind of petered out, even though we did do it eventually, except again, the audience was all people who were willing to stay after school to see it, whereas with *You Can't Take It With You* everyone got out of class so of course they liked it. And this one kid who's now a lawyer didn't even memorize his lines, I could have killed him, reading his lines out of the book while we were doing it, and today he makes more than us playwrights. I played Lucky, which is modest since it's a small part, but since I was also directing I wanted to keep my distance on it to make sure it was all kept stark and yet like vaudeville. I still remember the long speech of Lucky's, which is a tribute to you as a poet because when I recited it at home everyone thought it was gibberish. Here, I'll show you: *Given the existence as uttered forth in the public works of Puncher and Wattman of a personal God quaquaquaqua with white beard quaquaquaqua outside time without extension who from the heights of divine athambia divine aphasia loves us dearly with some exceptions for reasons unknown.*

Beckett: Stop, please, stop!

Interviewer: Oh, are you playing Vladimir? Don't jump the gun yet. —*fire the firmament that is to say blast hell to heaven so blue still and calm so calm*

Beckett: Please, I do know the speech, after all!

Interviewer: I guess it can be embarrassing to hear things you wrote thirty-five years ago read out loud. I used to write poems about the elves and fairies dancing around toadstools when I was in elementary school and if someone dragged them out now I would have a cow! Anyway, in addition to directing and playing Lucky I also made the poster, which was very stark, all lower case letters, except the Magic Marker smeared but we pretended it stood for the messiness of human suffering. Our drama teacher rolled his eyes and said at least he understood *You Can't Take It With You* and then he did it with two white kids playing Donald and Rheba and at the point where they're supposed to say, "Ever notice how white folks always getting themselves in trouble?" he had them say, "Ever notice how city folks always getting themselves in trouble?" They were supposed to be hillbillies. We did *Twelve Angry Women*, too, because there weren't enough boys interested in drama, they all said it was fruity. Is that a problem for you?

Beckett: I can't believe this is happening.

Interviewer: Interesting. Like your characters, you have a terror of reality.

Beckett: In this case.

Interviewer: You've written several novels, too. What are they like?

Beckett: I'm calling the police.

Interviewer: Careful, the cassette recorder isn't mine, I borrowed it!

Beckett: *(He does not speak.)*

Interviewer: You knew James Joyce. You did his typing and mail, I guess. Is there a simple explanation for *Finnegans Wake*, for people who know Joyce is great, but still? Remember, *simple*.

Beckett: *(He does not speak.)*

Interviewer: You're shaking a little. Shall I stand up and let you sit down?

Beckett: I can't go on like this.

Interviewer: "That's what you think!" Your writing is very apt, it's fun to quote.
Beckett: Please go.
Interviewer: You want me to go?
Beckett: Yes, please go.
Interviewer: *(He does not move.)*

OVERHEARD WHILE WALKING

"It was many, many years ago, at Lake Tahoe"
. . . "*I'm* inhibited?!" . . . "Your English *is*
improving! How much do you study?" "Two
days an hour" . . . "But Daddy doesn't *know* if
Michael Jackson is happy" . . . "Not a social*ist*—
a social*ite*" . . . "Honestly, a billion isn't as much
as it sounds" . . . "The Guggenheim *does* look
like a collapsible camp cup" . . . "You got
homeboys uptown, you got homeboys down-
town, you don't need me!" . . . "Spare change?

I'm trying to buy a condo" . . . "Is that the sun or the moon on your T-shirt?" . . . "I read about them in *Psychology Today*" . . . "An *iguana*? It just looks like a big old lizard to me!" . . . "I give up, why would you rather live on Mars than on Venus?" . . . "And I say to you, Einstein could not have gone to heaven, because he died an agnostic!" . . . "The Empire State Building is so tall, it actually *foreshortens itself* " . . . "Her parents are never supposed to find out he's a member of the Racquet Club" . . . "It *is* the fifty dollars, isn't it?" . . . "I have to go see my mother tonight." "Oh, what is she in?" . . . "Don't tell me what to do, you're not my pimp!" . . . "No, no—Betty is the *dog*" . . . "Did whoever wrote the 'Internationale' make any money off it?" . . . "I'm waiting for crack in a *spreadable* form" . . . "Ya, I haff been riding the subway all week, I feel very homely on it" . . . "I'm a normal person, I'm a normal person, I'm a normal person" . . . "It wasn't so long ago you would have said Ralph Lauren was yucky" . . . "Hey! Hey! You with the tie! Show me your résumé!" . . . "But Dalton is so *glitzy*" . . . "I should never have told the judges my cat tried to have sex with me" . . . "Call me the *following* fall, then" . . . "Look! 'Hot' Coffee! Why is hot in quotation marks?" . . . "There's someone who I know who I wish was dead" . . . "That's right, sweetie: *can-ta-loupe!*" . . . "I think

of myself as an executive who happens to swim"
. . . "She found she made twice as much in tips
if she wore a blond wig" . . . "Hey, Rambo—
shut up!" . . . "There *isn't* any Light Bulb District"
. . . "It's just Squeeze, not *the* Squeeze" . . . "And
they misspelled *jackals*" . . . "That kind of nudity
is so *insecure*" . . . "It just sort of steamrolled,
avalanched—what's the word? Snowballed" . . .
"No, just the opposite, performance artists are
people who *can't* sing, dance, *or* act" . . . " 'Only
the Best in Quality Spankography'—well, that's
a refreshing break from that anything-for-a-buck
stuff" . . . "I can hear you women saying, 'Oh, I
can't go to church, I don't have any skirts, all I
have are *pantsuits!*' Well, I have some news for
you ladies—you can *get* a skirt! It's not so hard
to get a skirt!" . . . "Its full name is Liberty
Enlightening the World. We rode the subway
right under it!" . . . "First of all, define *'history'* "
. . . "Hey, babe, what's your name? And where
are we going?"

THE WHOM OF KABOOM

OR WHAT HAPPENED

TO THE SHARK

———

For some reason, the Whom of Kaboom and his entourage came to our town. I guess they thought a failing waterfront would be fun. Anyway, he brought his yacht and invited Easel "Jack" Kovach to go on a cruise with him. He's that artist who did the infamous Venus de Mylar in front of City Hall. You know— that thing you have to walk all the way around to get past. Why a celebrity like Jack the Hipper should live in this dump, I don't know, but I once heard him say on the news he did it as a joke. When the Whom invited him Easel asked if he could bring a dozen friends, thinking that was a joke, too, so imagine his concealed surprise when the Whom instantly agreed.

The problem was, Easel had just published his tell-all autobiography, and now he didn't have a dozen friends. So, he invited a dozen people at random out of the phone book. It was supposed to be conceptual art, and even the Whom could appreciate the publicity that comes from charity. Anyway, I was invited, and so were some people you wouldn't want to meet. One you wouldn't mind meeting, but one you wouldn't remember meeting, was a little old lady named Reedy Wetwagon. She had never harmed anyone in her life, and to make sure, she never married or raised children. She was not only the most harmless but the oldest person on board, because the Whom may look dissipated, but he's youngish, and he likes a young staff, and even the yacht's captain was on his first command. Reedy didn't quite understand why she'd been invited, and I didn't either until my wife pointed out it was a joke, it was to mock me. Still, I decided to go on the cruise for the experience. And there was the possibility it might somehow be glamorous fun.

We set sail through a forest of flashbulbs. I was introduced to the Whom very briefly, but it was obvious we wouldn't spend any time with him or Easel Kovach. His assistant shook my hand for him, and the Whom asked me if I liked the skyline, but all I could think to say was that the new buildings looked like stacks of silver quarters. He smiled a little, and said that to him they looked like those peaked horns you see on demonic idols. That was the last I saw of him until the shark appeared.

The skyline, evil or not, soon disappeared from the horizon, and the caterers opened a perpetual buffet. The other random guests and I pretty much stationed ourselves there, except Reedy Wetwagon, who sat at the back of the dining room. She kept waiting for everyone to sit down, so she could fill her plate without jostling anyone, but the catering staff had to stand at the table at all times, and she didn't want to jostle them either, so she went unfed.

Meanwhile, according to our steward, the whole trip was a business expense. The Whom and Easel were having even more exceptional food in the Whom's cabin, where he was outlining a proposal to have Easel design a skyscraper in the shape of Kaboom itself. This would not have been easy, because I've seen Kaboom on the map and its borders are very ragged. The building, and Easel's fee, would have been colossal. Hundreds of rotating searchlights aimed in every direction would have been built into it, like X-ray eyes trying to see what was in the safe, or even where the safe was, and the traditional music of Kaboom would have been broadcast from hundreds of speakers at all times. The Whom said it was time our town knew what Kaboom sounded like. It sounds impressive, and I suppose there were a few janitorial jobs in it, but I still feel it was to make fun of our town. If it had been built, I don't suppose anyone here would ever have gotten any sleep again. Anyway, the steward said Easel seemed willing enough but admitted he was no architect, and pointed out that anything he designed might collapse or at least not support furniture or people. The Whom said it didn't have to, that the whole skyscraper could be hollow, no one would need to go inside it. It sounds more like a statue, but I wasn't there, so I don't grasp the fine points.

Just as the steward was telling us this gossip, a great storm arose, and the yacht was tossed in the mad maternal arms of the sea. The buffet table overturned and that started a panic. We heard a strange roar and we all ran out on deck. There in the water was the world's largest shark, and it began to demand a human sacrifice. I don't know what was more impressive, its enormous size, or that deep voice, but in the dementia of the storm it all seemed inevitable and natural. Apparently celebrities are attracted to each other, and when the Whom finally appeared on the upper deck, he shouted that he knew this shark. I guess they had met somewhere. He shook his combination scepter-phone at it and officially damned it, but he seemed to have no immediate power over it.

The dead-eyed fish kept on demanding a human sacrifice, as if it were responsible for the storm and could still the waters once it was fed. The Whom went back into his cabin, which I don't think he should have done, but at the time we assumed he was fetching a harpoon. The danger didn't seem to register with Easel, either, because he started taking photos of the shark. I guess they might have been for the police later, but I doubt you would have trouble picking it in a lineup. Unluckily for Reedy, the crew and most of the passengers were superstitious under their clean clothes, and crisis does bring out the craven and primitive. The captain, who really was too young, said in a jittery voice that it was a Jonah situation, and he called for straws to be drawn to see who would be thrown overboard. There were no straws on board, since this was a high-tech kind of yacht, so swizzle sticks were passed around, on the understanding that whoever got the least fancy one was to be God's choice for Jonah. As it happened, and I had my eyes closed the whole time, the old lady got the plainest swizzle stick, one with just a spherical knob at the end. Obviously, someone had to give it to her, but all I knew was that I had gotten one with a tiny pagoda that had pink elephants waving from its tiers, so I was safe.

Surprisingly, though I guess it made sense, Reedy Wetwagon didn't resist her selection. If she had, it might have caused an argument, and she also figured she really ought to pay for the cruise somehow, and it might as well be with her life. Chance had raised her high, so she owed it the favor of going when it sent her home. All she requested was that Easel do a sketch of her before she was thrown overboard. Even harmless types dream of immortality, and in her mind she may have thought its monetary value would help her somehow. He hadn't brought any materials with him, unfortunately, and even though the captain had pencils and chalk on the bridge, Easel didn't like them. The old lady herself had an Instamatic camera, however, and the famous artist offered to take her picture with it, since the fact that he had pressed the button would make people look at it. He took her picture, and she started to weep—over the attention, I guess, and the fact that she was to be thrown overboard.

The storm had continued to rage all this time, and the other guests got hysterical and shouted for the old woman to be thrown to the shark. They got violent about it, which I guess you should expect if you just pick twelve names at random out of the phone book to share times of crisis with. I admit I started screaming, but it wasn't anything about her. I never screamed anything about throwing her overboard. I just sort of screamed so no one would notice me.

Then the littlest of the caterers—who looked like an orphan with his bangs, and someone had said he was—slammed two serving trays together to get everyone's attention. He offered to carve a likeness of the old lady out of ice and throw it to the shark instead. He had already carved ice centerpieces for the buffet tables, mostly of eagles, swans ridden by figures of the Whom, and what was either a flat-topped dollar sign or a letter S, for Super, I guess. Anyway, Easel said that he could do a more memorable job than the caterer, even though ice wasn't his medium, but he pointed out that this shark was no fool, and if it could speak to make ultimatums, not to mention control the sea and the elements, then it probably knew ice from flesh and blood.

Suddenly the caterer grabbed a crate of after-dinner mints and threw them overboard, hoping to convince the shark that it had already eaten. You have to admire him, since he was small and everyone wanted to throw him to the shark if the old lady didn't work out. Maybe that's why he did it, but I'd like to think he was the baby she might have had and given up for adoption and she was the mother he never knew. She was way too old, I suppose, but I'm sentimental, and if they weren't related it's unclear why he was so persistent. He was crying, too, but to be fair his buffet had been overturned and he was soaking wet.

The shark swallowed the crate, all right, but the sugar rush from the mints only made it intensify its cries for a sacrifice, and it began to chant the old lady's name. It's funny, because everyone else on board certainly had more meat on them than she did, and the Whom is enormous, but the shark seemed to be looking forward to eating her, since she had been selected by fate, and sharks aren't necessarily above superstition themselves. It wanted what it had become convinced it had coming to it.

Then the little caterer threw the shark a tan-colored deck chair, hoping it would mistake it for a scrawny human sacrifice, but the shark knew better the moment it swallowed it. At last there was nothing to do but throw the old woman overboard, because the caterer had passed out after hurling the chair. One of the guests was an accountant and said Reedy had the least life to lose, so it was the best thing. I averted my eyes.

No sooner had she been tossed to the shark and swallowed than the mood on board became remorseful and more rational, a sort of postcoital enlightenment. The Whom finally emerged from his cabin and said he had just had to take an important phone call, but it was a secret and he couldn't tell us who had called. It reminded me that despite all their money, the people of Kaboom always depend on us to defend them. Everyone below realized that we had capitulated to the shark's demands too quickly, and since it was a talking shark, we wished we had tried to reason with it, to offer it money or other alternative booty mere dumb unspeaking fish would turn up their noselessness at. I had felt that way all along, but no one had asked me.

We all noticed that the storm still continued to rock the yacht. That was something else we hadn't considered. The shark had been bluffing. This got the Whom furious. He was angrier about the blow to his entrepreneurial pride than out of love for the old woman, who, with all respect, was a total stranger to him and too insipid for anyone to love deeply. The bad weather put him out of sorts, too. He shouted curses at the shark again, and spat into the water in challenge. Then he sent his bodyguards into the roiling icy waters to punish the shark for its misrepresentations and fraud. The little caterer regained consciousness and volunteered to go into the brine himself, but although no one discouraged him, the urge just sort of passed. There's still the possibility he was the old lady's lost son, or grandchild, anyway, even if they never realized it, and life does have magical near-misses as well as magical reunions.

Lightning writhed overhead like a dragon wracked by nightmares of monsters worse than itself, and thunder cracked like a nervous breakdown of the skies, offering a horrified accompaniment to the struggle. The bodyguards eventually hurled the falsifying shark onto the deck with us, where it thrashed and expired, despite the rain. Then they cut it open with a big knife from the Whom's own attaché case, and there was Reedy Wetwagon, among the license plates, anchors, and lost penknives. She was sitting in the tan-colored deck chair, which the shark's stomach acids had given a sort of tie-dyed look, and she herself was soggy but her hat was still on. She smiled and offered everyone after-dinner mints, which were only partially digested thanks to their plastic wrappers. Someone said she looked like an angel, but I think we were all edgy and eager for grace.

It would be nice to report at this point that the storm stopped, but in fact it continued for several hours, though it let up for a while and then got bad again for a few minutes. The shark really had been faking, and we all wondered how we ever could have believed a talking shark could do impossible things. The weather had calmed down, though, when the peaked horns of the city appeared like those of a clumsily concealed savage on the horizon. We all prepared to go our separate and even skewed ways.

Before we disembarked, though, one of the other passengers you wouldn't want to meet pointed out that this story had a happy ending and would make a good Movie of the Week called "A Woman Named Jonah." We all grinned, but in my heart I knew we were all guilty and that there was moral complexity in what had happened, so it wouldn't have been such a good Movie of the Week, even if it had the old lady slip overboard by accident. Besides, we had all signed releases promising not to speak to the press about the cruise or sell rights to our experience, because it was Easel's conceptual art idea and no one should make money on it but him. The caterers had already sworn to silence, since loose-lipped employees don't get asked back. I'm only telling you because I know no one listens to you. Also, there's some rule that the censors won't allow the Whom to be depicted by an actor. My wife says she would have liked to see me as played by a handsome man, but that might just have stirred up trouble at home.

So, it was back to my workaday grind at the Marine Prosthetics dock. As for the old woman, you remember her. She didn't want to be a bother, and the fact that she had survived loomed larger than that she had been nearly killed, so in a sense she did know something like nostalgia in her lifetime. I haven't heard from any of the others since then, except I sometimes read about Easel's coma and wonder whether that's a joke, too. The Whom certainly never came back, or built any skyscraper here, and I didn't even get to eat my fill on his cruise. That's my story, and I promise it's true, as sure as you and I are bound for Heaven. If you're no wiser for it, then either you or I must be to blame.

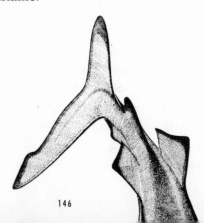